Y0-BEH-437

Loyola Marymount University
Los Angeles, California

Written by Kristin Cole
Edited by Abby Lyon, James Balzer

Additional contributions by Alissa Garcia, Adam Burns,
Omid Gohari, Christina Koshzow, Chris Mason, Kimberly Moore,
Joey Rahimi, Jon Skindzier, Luke Skurman, and Tim Williams

ISBN # 1-59658-076-3
ISSN # 1551-1087
© Copyright 2005 College Prowler
All Rights Reserved
Printed in the U.S.A.
www.collegeprowler.com

Special thanks to Babs Carryer, Andy Hannah, LaunchCyte, Tim O'Brien, Bob Sehlinger, Thomas Emerson, Andrew Skurman, Barbara Skurman, Bert Mann, Dave Lehman, Daniel Fayock, Chris Babyak,The Donald H. Jones Center for Entrepreneurship, Terry Slease, Jerry McGinnis, Bill Ecenberger, Idie McGinty, Kyle Russell, Jacque Zaremba, Larry Winderbaum, Paul Kelly, Roland Allen, Jon Reider, Team Evankovich, Julie Fenstermaker, Lauren Varacalli, Abu Noaman, Jason Putorti, Mark Exler, Daniel Steinmeyer, Jared Cohon, Gabriela Oates, Tri Ad Litho, David Koegler, and Glen Meakem.

Bounce Back Team: Faiza Mokhtar, Sarah Buser, Kim Berryman

College Prowler™
5001 Baum Blvd.
Suite 456
Pittsburgh, PA 15213

Phone: (412) 697-1390, 1(800) 290-2682
Fax: (412) 697-1396, 1(800) 772-4972
E-mail: info@collegeprowler.com
Website: www.collegeprowler.com

Welcome to College Prowler™

During the writing of College Prowler's guidebooks, we felt it was critical that our content was unbiased and unaffiliated with any college or university. We think it's important that our readers get honest information and a realistic impression of the student opinions on any campus — that's why if any aspect of a particular school is terrible, we (unlike a campus brochure) intend to publish it. While we do keep an eye out for the occasional extremist — the cheerleader or the cynic — we take pride in letting the students tell it like it is. We strive to create a book that's as representative as possible of each particular campus. Our books cover both the good and the bad, and whether the survey responses point to recurring trends or a variation in opinion, these sentiments are directly and proportionally expressed through our guides.

College Prowler guidebooks are in the hands of students throughout the entire process of their creation. Because you can't make student-written guides without the students, we have students at each campus who help write, randomly survey their peers, edit, layout, and perform accuracy checks on every book that we publish. From the very beginning, student writers gather the most up-to-date stats, facts, and inside information on their colleges. They fill each section with student quotes and summarize the findings in editorial reviews. In addition, each school receives a collection of letter grades (A through F) that reflect student opinion and help to represent contentment, prominence, or satisfaction for each of our 20 specific categories. Just as in grade school, the higher the mark the more content, more prominent, or more satisfied the students are with the particular category.

Once a book is written, additional students serve as editors and check for accuracy even more extensively. Our bounce-back team — a group of randomly selected students who have no involvement with the project — are asked to read over the material in order to help ensure that the book accurately expresses every aspect of the university and its students. This same process is applied to the 200-plus schools College Prowler currently covers. Each book is the result of endless student contributions, hundreds of pages of research and writing, and countless hours of hard work. All of this has led to the creation of a student information network that stretches across the nation to every school that we cover. It's no easy accomplishment, but it's the reason that our guides are such a great resource.

When reading our books and looking at our grades, keep in mind that every college is different and that the students who make up each school are not uniform — as a result, it is important to assess schools on a case-by-case basis. Because it's impossible to summarize an entire school with a single number or description, each book provides a dialogue, not a decision, that's made up of 20 different topics and hundreds of student quotes. In the end, we hope that this guide will serve as a valuable tool in your college selection process. Enjoy!

OMID GOHARI ◯ CHRISTINA KOSHZOW ◯ CHRIS MASON ◯ JOEY RAHIMI ◯ LUKE SKURMAN ◯
Founders of College Prowler™

Table of Contents

Introduction from the Author

To begin, Loyola Marymount University is not in Chicago, New Orleans, or Maryland. Never heard of it? It's okay, neither had I when I first moved to Los Angeles two years ago. When I began exploring my college possibilities, my choices seemed obvious: USC, UCLA, Pepperdine, maybe Cal State Northridge, or even California Lutheran. However, during my search, I stumbled across Loyola Marymount University. I checked the website, and it looked pretty, but I brushed it off and applied to the big name schools. Finally, on a whim, I applied to LMU on the last day after placing a frantic call to my high school guidance counselor to request my transcripts. Two days later, I received a letter of acceptance.

When people asked where I applied, I immediately responded, "USC, Pepperdine, and this little Catholic school, Loyola Marymount." I assumed that it was an unknown school, so I was shocked when even my relatives back east knew about LMU and its reputation as the "Ivy League of California."

LMU first won me over because of its appearance. I expected an urban school lodged firmly in the ghetto with concrete walls and graffiti. Instead, I saw the palm trees framing Sunken Garden and the bell tower that stands guard over all of the campus. The academics, the technology, and the students won me over later, and my last choice became my first choice. I wanted access to the film industry, but because I'm a small town girl at heart, I knew a giant university in the center of L.A. would intimidate me. LMU provides the access to L.A. when I need it and the escape from L.A. when I don't.

If you are exploring LMU, then you should know that the university is at a crossroads. The professors are emerging as nationally recognized experts, and our students are making strides in film, law, and business. If the goal is to become the "Georgetown of the West," then LMU is well on its way towards achieving this end. The university's identity represents a unique merger of Jesuit and Marymount philosophies, and the emphasis on education and service permeates every aspect of life as a Lion. It is a unique school designed to produce adults with unique ideas, interests, and goals.

Kristin Cole, Author
Loyola Marymount University

By the Numbers

General Information

Loyola Marymount University
1 LMU Drive
Los Angeles, CA
90045-2659

Control:
Private

Academic Calendar:
Semester

Religious Affiliation:
Roman Catholic (Jesuit and Marymount)

Founded:
1911

Website:
http://www.lmu.edu

Main Phone:
(310) 338-2700

Admissions Phone:
(310) 338-2750

Student Body

Full-Time Undergraduates:
5,312

Part-Time Undergraduates:
387

Full-Time Males:
2,306

Full-Time Females:
3393

Male to Female Ratio:
40% to 60%

Admissions

Overall Acceptance Rate:
59%

Total Applicants:
7,716

Total Acceptances:
4,568

Freshman Enrollment:
1,335

Yield (percentage of admitted students who actually enroll):
29%

Early Decision Available?
No

Early Action Available?
No

Regular Decision Deadline:
February 1

Regular Decision Notification:
Rolling

Must Reply-By Date:
May 1

Common Application Accepted?
No

Supplemental Forms?
Yes

Admissions Phone:
(310) 338-2750

Admissions E-mail:
admissions@lmu.edu

Admissions Website:http://www.lmu.edu/admissions

SAT I or ACT Required?
Either

First-Year Students Submitting SAT Scores:
95%

SAT I Range (25th – 75th Percentile):
1060-1250

SAT I Verbal Range (25th – 75th Percentile):
520-620

SAT I Math Range (25th – 75th Percentile):
540-630

SAT II Requirements for Bellarmine College of Liberal Arts:
Writing, One test selected by the applicant
SAT II Requirements for College of Business

Administration:
Writing, One test selected by the applicant (Math highly recommended.)

SAT II Requirements for College of Communication and Fine Arts:
Writing, One test selected by the applicant

SAT II Requirements for Frank R. Seaver College of Science and Engineering:
Writing, Biology, Chemistry, or Physics, Math I, Ic, or IIc

SAT II Requirements for School of Film and Television:
Writing, One test selected by the applicant

Retention Rate:
90%

Top 10% of High School Class:
30%

Application Fee:
$50

Applicants Placed on Waiting List:
731

Students Enrolled From Waiting List:
1

Transfer Applications Received:
1,199

Transfer Applications Accepted:
362

TransferStudents Enrolled:
223

Transfer Applicant Acceptance Rate:
19%

Financial Information

Tuition and Fees:
$25,744

Room and Board:
$9,456

Books and Supplies:
$832

Average Need-Based Financial Aid Package (including loans, work-study, grants, and other sources):
$23,800

Students Who Applied For Financial Aid:
80%

Students Who Applied For Financial Aid and Received It:
78%

Financial Aid Forms Deadline:
The FAFSA and PROFILE are due by February 15. Copies of tax returns are due by April 16.

Financial Aid Phone:
(310) 338-2753

Financial Aid E-mail:
finaid@lmu.edu

Financial Aid Website:
http://www.lmu.edu/pages/1149.asp

Academics

The Lowdown On...
Academics

Degrees Awarded:
Bachelor's
Master's
Doctorate

Most Popular Areas of Study:
Business 26%
Film Production 7%
Communications 7%
Psychology 7%

Undergraduate Schools:
Bellarmine College of Liberal Arts
College of Business Administration
College of Communication and Fine Arts
Frank R. Seaver College of Science and Engineering
School of Film and Television

Fulltime Faculty:
419

Faculty with Terminal Degree:
62%

Student-to-Faculty Ratio:
13:1

Average Course Load:
Five

Dual-Degree Programs:
LMU allows for double majoring in all colleges.

Special MBA Options:
Executive MBA

Comparative Management Systems Program

Systems Engineering Leadership Program (a dual MS and MBA)

Juris Doctorate MBA (with Loyola Law School)

Teacher Certification

Journalism Certificate

University Honors Program

AFROTC-Aerospace Studies Program

Marital and Family Therapy Program

Master of Arts in Bioethics (New for Fall 2005)

Best Places to Study:
Library

Lion's Den

The Pond

Sample Academic Clubs:
Accounting Society

Alpha Psi Omega

Alpha Sigma Nu

American Society of Civil Engineers

Animation Club

Business Law Society

Chicanos for Creative Medicine

Economics Society

Latino Business Student Association

National Society of Black Engineers

Psi Chi

Sigma Tau Delta

Society of Women Engineers

Tri Beta Biological Honors Society

Graduation Rate...
Four Year: 62%

Five Year: 71%

Six Year: 70%

AP Test Score Requirements
Possible credit for scores of 4 or 5

IB Test Score Requirements
Possible credit for scores of 6 or 7

Did You Know?

Class actually can be fun at LMU! The School of Film and Television offers FILM 398: Nintendo Narratives as an elective.

In the April 1, 2003 education column of The Washington Post, **writer Jay Mathews** names LMU among 100 universities that deserve greater recognition.

Entrepreneur magazine ranked LMU's Entrepreneurship Program among the **Top 10 out of 825** programs nationally.

Add: For creative students, **LMU offers majors in Recording Arts, Screenwriting, Animation, and Multimedia Arts**, along with a full range of Fine Arts Programs.

Check out unusual minors like **Archaeology**, Irish Studies, or Ethics to broaden your prespective.

Students Speak Out On...
Academics

"There were some teachers that were awesome. Most of my classes were interesting, especially Epic and Biology Lab, but the others were just your routine intro classes, so not much excitement there."

Q "Like all the schools I have attended, there are teachers I love and teachers I hate. I don't think you can ever escape that. The classes were weird for me at first, because I was used to having a test all the time. But **you get used to the midterm and final routine**. I think it makes the classes better because I hate to study, and I can concentrate on learning. I love going to class at LMU even if I don't like the teacher so much. I feel that I really do learn. I think they are interesting because you can choose from your core what classes most interest you, and, of course, your major should interest you, too."

Q "The teachers at LMU are **devoted to teaching each and every student** until they get it. Though you will occasionally run into the psycho how-did-they-ever-get-a-job-here teachers, they are caring, for the most part."

Q "The teachers, I must say, are overall **helpful, concerned, and considerate.** I truly believe that they want each student to leave their class with a fuller and more genuine feeling and understanding for the field of study in which they teach."

Q "Most teachers are helpful and willing to help you understand the information presented in class. There are teachers who are **extremely passionate about the material they teach.** In all the classes I have taken, professors made an effort to know my name, rather than my social security number, as well as to get to know me better as a student and a person. Most importantly, they are accessible for office hours. In addition, most professors are extremely easygoing and can talk to them about anything."

Q "Before coming to LMU, I received a DVD in the mail containing interviews with the professors, and I was a bit concerned at how young they all seemed. I have been pleasantly surprised, however. Most of the professors at LMU have a Ph.D. or are currently working towards one. My specific professors are mostly good, and it seems as though they average out; I have one who is a Yale-educated, highly intellectual woman and another who is **about as sharp as the broad side of a cello**. About half of the classes I've taken I find genuinely interesting, while the other half I find purposeless."

Q "In general, all the teachers are extremely accessible and really nice. Many are **aware of the stresses we students face** and are willing to work with us when it comes to deadlines. Others are less lenient, but certainly don't have expectations that are too high or impossible. Some classes were more interesting than others."

Q "**LMU seems hard.** I have to study my butt off to get an A in a class. It's not that the work at LMU is any more challenging, but it seems like I am getting more busy work."

Q "**LMU's difficulty level depends on how much you put into it,** and how much self worth and self desire you have to succeed. If you just want to slide by, then you have all semester to do whatever you wish, and then the night before midterms and finals, cram."

Q "I'd say that **I liked most of my professors**. Some professors are terrible, but you can avoid them easily, especially when it comes to your core classes."

Q "I had a history professor who never gave above an A-, but that's the only time I ever felt like a professor was out to get her students. Most professors want their students to succeed and are **willing to give you a break if you need extra time.**"

The College Prowler Take On...
Academics

According to the school's mission statement, academics at LMU focus on "the education of the whole person." Professors at LMU must subscribe to the university's mission statement, so most professors welcome students' opinions and recognize students' differences. The student-professor relationship encourages a free exchange of ideas. The courses, especially the core curriculum, allow students to customize their education by selecting from a wide array of classes to fulfill requirements in critical and creative arts, history, theology, philosophy, social sciences, and mathematics.

LMU's strength is in the strong relationship between students and professors. They are available via e-mail, phone, and office hours. Most professors respond to students' questions within hours. Students are more than just a social security number; professors usually learn their students' names after the first class, and a few take photos of their students. Plagiarism of any kind causes serious consequences at LMU, including expulsion. It doesn't pay to cheat; most professors take it very personally. Also, bad professors stand out, and word travels fast around campus about whom to avoid.

On the negative side, the attendance policy is usually very strict. A few professors do not take attendance, but most do. In most departments, students can miss three classes before their grade drops. Attendance and class participation count for at least ten percent of the final grade. Additionally, LMU's academics are strangely lacking in some areas. For instance, there is no journalism major, only a journalism certificate. In the next several years, LMU will eliminate its African-American Studies, Women's Studies, Asian Pacific Studies, and Chicano/Latino Studies and combine them all under one major: American Cultures. It is a move that differs from other universities.

Although the strict attendance policy can seem intimidating, most classes at LMU are worth attending. Combine an exciting professor with an interesting subject, and you are guaranteed to learn.

The College Prowler™ Grade on
Academics: B

A high Academics grade generally indicates that professors are knowledgeable, accessible, and genuinely interested in their students' welfare. Other determining factors include class size, how well professors communicate, and whether or not classes are engaging.

Local Atmosphere

The Lowdown On...
Local Atmosphere

Region:
West

City, State:
Los Angeles, California

Setting:
Suburban

Distance from Downtown Los Angeles:
25 Minutes

Distance from San Diego:
2.5 Hours

Distance from Las Vegas:
5.5 Hours

Points of Interest:
Disneyland
Six Flags Magic Mountain
Knott's Berry Farm
Griffith Park

Universal Studios Hollywood
La Brea Tar Pits
Universal City Walk
Grauman's Chinese Theatre
Getty Center
Los Angeles Zoo
Chinatown
Dodger Stadium
Museum of Tolerance
Hollywood Bowl
Museum of Contemporary Art
Museum of Neon Art
Heritage Square Museum
Little Tokyo
Autry Museum of Western
Heritage
California Science Center
Exposition Park
Staples Center
Skirball Cultural Center
Santa Monica Pier
Malibu
The beach!
The Grove

Closest Shopping Malls or Plazas:
Westfield Shoppingtown Fox
Hills
Westfield Shoppingtown Century City
Third Street Promenade in
Santa Monica
Marina Marketplace
Promenade at Howard Hughes
Center

Closest Movie Theatres:

United Artists Cinema 6
4335 Glencoe Ave., Marina del
Rey
Phone:
(310) 823-1721

Loews Marina Marketplace
13455 Maxella Ave. Suite 270,
Marina del Rey
Phone:
(310) 827-7955

Loews Broadway Cinemas 4
1441 Third Street Promenade,
Santa Monica
Phone:
(310) 458-6232

The Bridge:
Cinema de Lux
6081 Center Dr., Los Angeles
Phone:
(310) 568-3375

Major Sports Teams:
Dodgers (baseball)
Anaheim Angels (baseball)
Lakers (basketball)
Mighty Ducks (hockey)

Did You Know?

5 Fun Facts about Los Angeles:

- **The city's full name is** El Pueblo de Nuestra Senora la Reina de los Angeles de Porciuncula (The Town of the Queen of the Angels.)

- Los Angeles has the **largest number of women-owned businesses** in the nation.

- **Love the movies**? While living in Los Angeles, you may appear in one. Freeways, pedestrian malls, and restaurants are prime targets for filming.

- Los Angeles is the **birthplace of the Internet**, Mickey Mouse, Barbie, the DC-3, the Mazda Miata, and the Space Shuttle.

- Marina del Rey has **the largest manmade recreational harbor** and houses more than 6,000 yachts.

Famous People from Los Angeles:

Although many celebrities now call Los Angeles home, these famous people are true Angelenos:

- Shirley Temple
- Julia Child
- Coolio
- Leonardo DiCaprio
- Theodore Harold Maiman
- Mark McGwire
- Isamu Noguchi
- Robert Redford
- Sally Ride
- William Saroyan
- Adlai Stevenson
- Earl Warren
- Serena and Venus Williams
- Myra Wilson
- Tiger Woods

City Websites:

http://www.ci.la.ca.us/
http://www.losangeles.com
http://www.at-la.com
http://losangeles.areaguides.net

Local Slang

Know your numbers! The 405, 5, 10, 90, 210, 101, 110, and 14 are all Los Angeles freeways that connect various parts of the city.

Marine layer/sea fog: a thick cloud of heavy fog that rolls in over the coast after sunset and stays until shortly after sunrise

The Fu: what LMU students call the Furama Hotel in Westchester, which the university uses for temporary student housing

The Industry: the entertainment industry

Westside: LMU is in Los Angeles' trendy Westside that includes Beverly Hills, Marina del Rey, Malibu, and Hollywood.

Students Speak Out On...
Local Atmosphere

"Great town! Lots to do, museums, shopping, sports events, and, of course, the beach! Other universities are in fairly close proximity to LMU. There is always an element of danger anywhere, but the Los Angeles is a haven of good and bad. Be cautious and never let your guard down."

Q "This is LA! LMU is near UCLA and USC. You're next to Venice Beach! You're near Hollywood. There's nowhere better to be. This is the place to visit. Besides all that, LMU is beautiful. You are on a bluff overlooking a beautiful view. **The classes are small.** The dorms are big and spacious. Grass and trees are everywhere. We're also very close to LAX! **We even have a wonderful religious community and beautiful church**. And for all those religious people—our school is in the shape of a cross. In my opinion there is no better place to be!"

Q "Westchester is great. **It's very safe, pretty small, and the people are nice**—yet it's right in LA, where all the great stuff is. Unlike USC (University of Southern California), LMU is certainly not in a bad area, and I have never felt unsafe there. There are no other universities in Westchester other than LMU that I am aware of. I love taking walks around LMU and going to the little restaurants there, driving down to Marina del Rey and Santa Monica, and going to all the great malls and shopping centers nearby."

Q "L.A. is wonderful. When I first came to Los Angeles from Omaha, **I thought that the people would be phony,** cold-shouldered, and criminals. I have experienced quite the opposite. People in Los Angeles have actually been much nicer to me than in Omaha. They are infinitely more interesting to talk to, and there is an excellent variety of ethnicities and races. Of course, there are plenty of other universities present. In fact, just down the street from LMU is Otis College, and not far away is Santa Monica City College, widely considered as the best community college in the country. Two very popular schools, UCLA and USC, also make Los Angeles their home, with a combined enrollment of over 50,000. On the other hand, coming to Los Angeles meant that I would have to take extra precautions with security. Driving or walking through Compton or Watts late at night is still a little nerve-wracking. **Some of the more negative influences around Los Angeles convene in the shadows of Hollywood**. At a dance club, my friends had their car stolen from a parking lot, and it isn't uncommon to see ambulances storming through the middle of Sunset."

Q "Los Angeles is actually not a terribly evil town. **Hollywood is a very fascinating place to visit.** There is the obligatory Hollywood Walk of Fame or the famous sign, but more intriguing are the people you'll run into in some of the tiny shops or restaurants. Go into one of the many late-night diners if you're in Hollywood after midnight. If meeting unusual people interests you, another place to visit in Los Angeles is the Venice Beach boardwalk. I, like most of the tourists on the boardwalk, was completely culture-shocked when I saw such odd behavior and folk."

Q "LMU is a in a good location, not too deep in the city or completely away from it. It is also minutes from LAX, which does not pose that much of a problem. LMU is relatively close to UCLA in Westwood, USC in downtown Los Angeles, Pepperdine in Malibu, and Otis Art College literally minutes away from LMU. **The atmosphere in Westchester is pretty lively** especially because it is near Marina del Rey and situated in the Westside."

Q "There is so much to do, such as going to the many beaches in the area. Also, there is a plethora of shopping malls to indulge your interests. In addition, Los Angeles is such a diverse city which makes it all the more interesting, especially in downtown Los Angeles, such as Little Toyko, Olivera Street, Chinatown, etc. Of course, **there is Hollywood and the famous Sunset Strip!** The only place to stay away from is Hollywood and Sunset in the late hours, unless you want to be solicited by a working girl/guy."

Q "**The town is not a college town.** It's a residential area on one side and the back of an airport on the other that has a mix of minivans and wandering travelers. LMU seems sort of out of place in Westchester, but it's L.A. It's not as though you really have to stay within the ten blocks that surround campus."

Q "There are a million and one things to do in L.A., no matter what your scene. Rent a sailboat in the marina for a few hours, then do lunch or dinner at Tony P's or The Cheesecake Factory. There is a theater district in North Hollywood and a lot of LMU students are in plays there. Go see them! They have **cheap student tickets**, too!"

Q "If you are into cars, there is the Petersen Automotive Museum at 6060 Wilshire Blvd. in Fairfax. **I had a blast** at that place, plus student discounts rock, and you can get in for $5. There are 150 race cars, classic cars, hot rods, and movie cars like the Batmobile and the Green Hornet."

The College Prowler Take On...
Local Atmosphere

Say "Los Angeles," and many people conjure up images of catastrophic earthquakes, wildfires, and Rodney King. However, this city wears a variety of faces; neighborhoods change within miles, and many types of people occupy Los Angeles' vast territory. Los Angeles is not always synonymous with ghetto, nor is the entire city like Beverly Hills. In fact, the real charm of Los Angeles comes from the various cultures, classes, and people that form the city.

Loyola Marymount University also wears multiple faces. The university prides itself on being simultaneously part of L.A., yet separate from it. LMU is close to the culture and nightlife that makes L.A. so unique, but the university lacks the crime and concrete of the city. The university has a Los Angeles address, but the campus sits in Westchester, a quiet suburb in the western half of Los Angeles. Drive a few miles west of campus and enjoy the crashing waves of the Pacific; drive a few miles northeast and join the busy, crazy city. L.A. and LMU can satisfy any mood or any personality.

Los Angeles offers its visitors first-class shopping, food, and entertainment. Big spenders should check out the trendy shops on Rodeo Drive, a favorite haunt of celebrities. For more unique fare, Venice features tiny shops peddling one-of-a-kind clothing and antiques. Third Street Promenade in Santa Monica, a huge pedestrian mall, houses the most popular chain stores like Abercrombie and Fitch, Armani Exchange, and Gap. While shopping, stop at any number of restaurants like The Cheesecake Factory or The Chart House in Marina del Rey. For less money, there is always a Johnny Rockets or Islands nearby.

A

The College Prowler™ Grade on

Local
Atmosphere: A

A high Local Atmosphere grade indicates that the area surrounding campus is safe and scenic. Other factors include nearby attractions, proximity to other schools, and the town's attitude toward students

Safety & Security

The Lowdown On...
Safety & Security

Number of LMU Public Safety Officers:
The exact number is confidential.

Phone:
(310)338-2893(non-emergency)
222 (on-campus emergency)

Safety Services:
Bicycle registration
Property engraving
Information booth
Gated entrances
Emergency blue phones
Safety seminars (disaster pre-paredness
Theft prevention
Rape prevention
Campus safety
Safe ride home
Student escort service
Emt
Vehicle assistance

Health Services:

Treatment for illnesses and injuries

Women's health services

Dermatological care

Medications

Immunizations

Allergy shots

Lab work

X-rays

Orthopedic clinic

STD testing

Pregnancy testing

Balanced living seminars

Psychological and drug counseling

Health Center Office Hours:

Monday through Friday 8 a.m.-5 p.m. and Wednesday 8 a.m.-7 p.m.

Did You Know?

On April 26, 2004, **construction crews nearby unearthed two World War II-era explosive casings**, forcing LMU to evacuate half of the campus. The school canceled classes for the day, and LMU students responded in characteristic fashion: campus bands gave an impromptu concert, and students put aside their books to play Frisbee as the police helicopters hovered overhead.

In Fall 2004, a series of incidents involving vandalism and racial slurs rocked the LMU campus. Students responded by hosting a protest march and anti-discrimination rally. The LAPD is still investigating the incidents.

Students Speak Out On...
Safety & Security

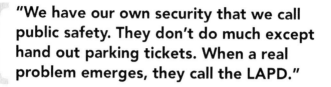

"We have our own security that we call public safety. They don't do much except hand out parking tickets. When a real problem emerges, they call the LAPD."

Q "Well, it's not Fort Knox, but **I've felt pretty safe.**"

Q "It's really, really great. I never feel unsafe. The security people always seem constantly on top of everything that happens on our small campus, right down to illegal parking. I left my car illegally parked for no more than twenty minutes, and when I came back, it already had a hefty ticket. They also have **twenty-four hour escort service** and all the nice things a campus should have."

Q "Security on campus is **top-notch.** After having visited other campuses and seeing their systems, it is reasonable to say that LMU has an excellent Public Safety team. With a late-night escort service, manned security gates, and 24-hour patrolling, there is absolutely no reason to feel insecure at LMU."

Q "For the most part, LMU is relatively safe. There have been many times where I walk around at night and never have to worry for my safety or if something horrible will happen to me. As for security, Public Safety, **all I see them do is giving parking** tickets all the time and drive around campus exceeding the posted speed limits. Actually, they have escorts, in the case you are uneasy walking around campus at night and can drive you back to dorm rooms."

Q "I once saw a homeless woman gathering up and eating the stray French fries on the countertops at the Lair. It made me question the security a bit but it wasn't like an everyday occurrence. The campus has always felt **very friendly, clean, safe and secure,** except that day."

Q "Public Safety at LMU truly provides **a secure and stable program** and makes you feel comfortable and at home with their policies and cautionary procedures when it comes to safety."

Q **"It's a safe campus, especially for L.A.** I almost went to USC, and that place is right in the middle of a ghetto."

Q "Campus safety is okay, but I think **Public Safety just writes out parking tickets."**

The College Prowler Take On...
Safety & Security

Unlike other Los Angeles universities, LMU does not need the security measures of a military base to keep students safe. There are two entrances: the main entrance off Lincoln Blvd. and a second entrance at Loyola Blvd. A security booth stands at the gated front entrance to the campus, but the gate remains open during the day. The back entrance off of Loyola Blvd. offers access to the visitor parking lot, but there are no guards controlling access to the campus. The light security at the entrances allows people from the surrounding neighborhoods to walk on to campus, but occasionally it also lets in a few shady characters. However, public safety's red trucks patrol the campus constantly. If a serious problem develops, they call the LAPD.

Traffic regulations on campus are strict, so one of the public safety officers' main duties is to issue parking tickets. They frequently respond to reports of underage drinking or minor thefts, but students cause virtually all of these incidents. There are also occasional incidents of harassment between students, but only a few cases of assault in the university's history. The flaw in LMU security is in the gated entrances. Anyone can enter the campus on foot, and usually, guards at the security booth do not stop cars that do not have a university parking permit. Overall, students do not worry about physical safety because serious or violent crime is almost non-existent.

B

The College Prowler™ Grade on

Safety & Security:
B

A high grade in Safety & Security means that students generally feel safe, campus police are visible, blue-light phones and escort services are readily available, and safety precautions are not overly necessary.

Computers

The Lowdown On...
Computers

High-Speed Network?
Yes

Wireless Network?
Yes

Number of Labs:
13

24-Hour Labs:
None

Numbers of Computers:
Several hundred.

Free Software:
Adobe Acrobat

Operating Systems
PC, Mac. Most computers run on Windows XP, but some have Windows ME or Windows 2000.

Charge to Print?
Yes, ten cents per page.

Discounted Software
Software at student discounts is available at the campus bookstore or online at http://www.efollett.com.
- Microsoft Office Standard: $149.98
- Microsoft Office Professional: $149.98
- Symantec Systemworks: $79.98
- Norton Antivirus: $32.98
- MATLAB: $99.98
- MCH Multimedia Software: $39.98

Did You Know?

LMU recently expanded its wireless network to include most locations on campus, including the Atrium in University Hall, the library, and more.

Students Speak Out On...
Computers

> **"The lab in the library is always crowded, usually in the afternoons, but there's the St. Rob's lab which is more reliable and Perriera, but it's too small. It would be helpful to bring your own computer** because there are also Ethernet connections around campus.**"**

Q "The computer labs aren't really crowded except during convo hour, but there are plenty of labs where you can always find something available. **The labs don't have color ink,** though. Yes, you should bring your own computer because it's easier and because we have fast and free internet in the rooms!"

Q "The computer lab in the library always has lots of people on it, but **I have never had to wait for a computer;** there's usually at least one that's open. The other labs, such as the learning and animation labs, have plenty of computers and only about three or four people there at a time, making for a convenient, quiet study environment."

Q "The computer network provides high-speed Internet access across campus and recently **wireless Internet access in limited locations.** The computer labs have their peak hours from noon to 6 p.m., except on Fridays. On Fridays, you'll always be able to get a computer in the computer lab because the campus is completely deserted."

Q "**You should bring a computer** preferably a laptop, because when you need to use a computer on campus the most, chances are everyone else will feel the same way. Bringing a laptop allows more storage for your information and documents."

Q "The computer network is fast when it's working, bu**t the network gets 'temporarily shut down for repair'** at inconvenient times."

Q "Computer labs are **always accessible and never too crowded.** To have your own computer is always a plus!"

Q "Everyone brings their own computer, but **the computer labs are still pretty crowded.** If you're a film student, by your sophomore year, you'll need a Mac."

Q "If you can't afford a computer, don't worry. **There are tons of computers all over campus.** I always go into the Sociology village computer lab because it's usually empty. The only problem is that the printers sometimes don't work in the labs."

Q "The labs are fine. I hate the e-mail and Internet here, though. **They don't do anything to stop viruses**, so I get like three e-mails a day with viruses. Plus, they're always repairing the network at the weirdest times, and it's always during finals or midterms."

The College Prowler Take On...
Computers

Got a project due and your computer crashed? Visit one of LMU's numerous computer labs around campus. The main computer labs in St. Roberts or the basement floor of the library house approximately twenty-five computers each that offer the full Microsoft Office suite. Labs get crowded, especially towards the end of the semester, and the charge for printing adds up quickly. The labs are nice for group projects, but for a last-minute paper, you are better off with your own computer and printer to avoid competition for a spot in the labs. If you need to use one of the computer labs, it might be worth it to try the smaller labs in University Hall. Although they are open for very limited hours, for most of the semester, these labs tend to be empty and quiet.

One word of caution when using the LMU computer network: The system is shut down for maintenance often—usually at the most inconvenient times. Viruses also run rampant through the system and attack users through e-mail. Often, users receive three e-mails a day containing viruses, so use an antivirus software and keep up to date with warnings about the latest virus on campus.

The College Prowler™ Grade on

Computers: B-

A high grade in Computers designates that computer labs are available, the computer network is easily accessible, and the campus' computing technology is up-to-date.

Facilities

The Lowdown On...
Facilities

Bowling on Campus?
No

Bar on Campus?
The Bird's Nest serves alcohol, but is a multipurpose gathering place for campus events.

Coffeehouse on Campus?
The Lion's Den in Malone Center

Lion's Corner Café in University Hall

The coffee cart at the Pond.

Student Center:
Malone Student Center.

Athletic Center:
Burns Recreation Center
Gersten Pavillion

Libraries:
1

Campus Size:
120 acres

What Is There to Do?

The LMU campus offers something for everyone. The gym at Burns Rec Center features modern equipment, including treadmills with individual cable televisions and a wide range of weight machines. The center also offers table tennis, swimming, exercise classes, tennis, and basketball. In the mood for caffeine? LMU features three coffee shops with a variety of espresso, cappuccino, and tea to satisfy the caffeine craving. Students also can join an intramural sport on Hannon Field before dinner and then grab a late-night dessert at The Lion's Den before dark. The Living Room features poetry readings, music, and comedy from talented students. For something really unique, view a mummified kitten from Egypt or a Buddah statue from Afganistan at the campus archeology museum

Movie Theatre on Campus?

Yes. Mayer Theatre shows weekly movies open to film students only. Associated Students of LMU also shows movies in St. Robert's Auditorium.

Favorite Things to Do

LMU's School of Film and Television ensures that good movies are shown frequently. The school also welcomes many celebrity guest speakers and private screenings. LMU also features prominent musicians in intimate concert settings, while theatre arts students perform controversial plays like The Vagina Monologues to a crowded auditorium. Aside from its many speakers and forums, LMU also offers plenty of open space for Frisbee, lacrosse, or just laying out in the sun. Convo Hour (Tuesdays and Thursdays from 12 p.m.-1:30 p.m.) often features barbeques, music, and guest speakers. Free food always draws a large crowd.

Popular Places to Chill

Sunken Garden is perfect for Frisbee, while the courtyard in front of the quad is a popular tanning spot. The Pond between Foley and Seaver offers a peaceful spot to drink coffee and talk. The Lion's Den offers loud music and giant social gatherings in between classes.

Students Speak Out On...
Facilities

"Well, the rec center looks nice from the outside. I feel ashamed for not actually going inside to work out. The computers in the computer lab in the library are nice, and Internet connections are fast. The library needs to expand, though. Too many books and not enough space."

"**We have a gorgeous gym**. The Lakers even come to LMU's gym to practice."

"LMU is beautiful. Everything is made **nice and comfy.**"

"The facilities are **absolutely awesome and modern.** The gym has many modern machines (more than just your basic treadmills), including jacks for headphones, which let you watch the TV's! A gym with four TV's is totally awesome. The student centers, such as the Lion's Den, are great places to hang out, relax, read, get coffee, and talk to people. I definitely have no complaints about the facilities."

"The gym is awesome! **The equipment at the gym is completely top of the line.** There is a variety of equipment in gym, not just limited to thousands of treadmills and free weights. The student center is pretty good. There is always someone who can help you out with anything."

Q "**There is a center for first-year students,** which has helped me a lot with any questions I had and made college bearable and doable. Most of the computers are up-to-date with some few exceptions like in the engineering computer lab. The computers there are Windows 98 powered, but most computers around campus are powered by Windows 2000 and Windows XP with the complete package of the Microsoft Office suite."

Q "The facilities are beautiful. You'll know where your tuition goes when you step into the gym, the computer labs, or sit by the trickling fountain in the fully stocked library. **You always see people doing maintenance on campus,** gardening and painting and repairing to keep it gorgeous."

Q "All on campus facilities are **nice and well kept**. However, West Hall could use a little help in the classrooms and the restrooms!"

Q "Most buildings are nice. University Hall is great, but **the dining halls are kind of gross**. Some of the dorms could use work, like Rosecrans and Whelan."

Q "They put a ton of money into the buildings here, except for West Hall. **I always feel like the walls will collapse in an earthquake.**"

The College Prowler Take On...
Facilities

Facilities at LMU fall into two categories: new and old. New buildings like University Hall, Burns Rec Center, and dorms like Rains and McCarthy feature bright, modern architecture with lots of natural light. On the other side of the coin are the older buildings like Seaver, the library, and dorms like McKay and Whelan. These buildings have uninspired, bland architecture, but the interior matches the same level of quality and cleanliness found in the newer buildings. All classrooms are large and comfortable; they feature a projection system, computer, Internet, and cable. To keep the rooms nice, signs forbid students from eating and drinking in the classrooms, but the rules are rarely enforced. Overall, the entire campus is extremely clean. The university employs a huge staff to maintain the plants and clean the classrooms. The maintenance staff even cleans the sidewalks and dusts the escalators.

The campus eyesore is West Hall, a small set of portable classrooms near Leavey and Xavier. These rooms are hot and dark, and the bathrooms in the adjacent trailer are miniscule. Students complain frequently about this building because it is often neglected. Among the other big, beautiful buildings on campus, West Hall simply does not fit in.

The College Prowler™ Grade on

A high Facilities grade indicates that the campus is aesthetically pleasing and well-maintained; facilities are state-of-the-art, and libraries are exceptional. Other determining factors include the quality of both athletic and student centers and an abundance of things to do on campus.

Campus Dining

The Lowdown On...
Campus Dining

Freshman Meal Plan Requirement?

Yes, for on-campus freshman

Meal Plan Average Cost:

$2,587

Note:

All places on campus accept cash, in addition to LIONS and Flexi-Dollars.

Places to Grab a Bite with Your Meal Plan

Hotdog Cart

Location: Southwest Corner of McCarthy Hall

Food: American

Favorite Dish: Hot dog, Chips, Fruit

Hours: Monday-Thursday 11 a.m.-3:30 p.m., Friday from 11 a.m.-2:30 p.m.

Accepts: LIONS and Flexi-dollars

Jamba Juice

Location: Malone Center next to Lair Marketplace

Food: Shakes and Smoothies

Favorite Dish: Peach Pleasure Smoothie

Hours: Monday-Thursday 7:30 a.m.-9:30 p.m., Friday 7:30 a.m.-9:30 p.m., Saturday 9:30 a.m.-9 p.m., and Sunday 9:30 a.m.-9:30 p.m.

Accepts: LIONS and Flexi-dollars

Lion's Café

Location: Alumni Mall between Foley and Seaver

Food: Pastries, Bagels, Coffee

Favorite Dish: Everything Bagel and a Mocha Bianca

Hours: Monday-Thursday 7:30 a.m.-9:30 p.m., Friday 7:30 a.m.-5 p.m.

Accepts: LIONS and Flexi-dollars

The Lair Marketplace

Location: Malone Student Center

Food: American, Mexican, Asian, Italian

Favorite Dish: Fettucine Alfredo, Pizza, Bean Burrito

Hours: Monday-Thursday 7:30 a.m.-12:30 a.m., Friday 7:30 a.m.-9 p.m., Saturday 8 a.m.-9 p.m., Sunday 10 a.m.-10 p.m.

Accepts: LIONS and Flexi-dollars

The Lion's Corner Café

Location: University Hall

Food: Pastries, Organic Coffee, Salads, and Sandwiches

Favorite Dish: Honey Almond Cheese Croissant, Cookies

Hours: Monday-Thursday 7:30 a.m. to 9:30 p.m. and Friday 7:30 a.m. to 5 p.m.

Accepts: LIONS and Flexi-dollars

The Lion's Den

Location: Malone Center

Favorite Dish: Vanilla Chai, Mocha

Hours: Varies

Accepts: LIONS and Flexi-dollars

Roski Dining Hall

Location: University Hall

Food: American, Italian, Mexican

Favorite Dish: Sandwiches from Boar's Head, Pizza, Chicken Tostada

Hours: Monday-Thursday 8:30 a.m.-7:30 p.m., Friday 8:30 a.m.-3:30 p.m.

Accepts: LIONS and Flexi-dollars

Off-Campus Places to Use Your Meal Plan:

Beach Pizza

Address: 8115 W. Manchester Ave., Playa del Rey

Beach Pizza (Continued....)
Phone: (310) 827-2000
Location: Playa del Rey
Food: Pizza
Favorite Dish: Pepperoni Pizza
Hours: Sunday-Thursday 11
a.m.-10 p.m., Friday-Saturday
11 a.m.-11 p.m.
Accepts: Flexi-dollars only

Chipotle Mexican Grill
Address: 4718 Admiralty Way,
Marina del Rey
Phone: (310) 821-0059
Location: Marina del Rey
Food: Mexican
Favorite Dish: Vegetarian Fajita
Burrito
Hours: Daily 11 a.m.-10 p.m.
Accepts: Flexi-dollars only

Domino's Pizza
Address: 8320 Lincoln Blvd.,
Westchester
Phone: (310) 216-6886
Location: Los Angeles
Food: Pizza
Favorite Dish: Buffalo Wings,
Pizza, Amazin' Greens Salad
Hours: Daily 11 a.m.-11 p.m.
Accepts: LIONS meal plan and
Flexi-dollars

Hank's Pizza
Address: 442 W. Manchester
Ave., Playa del Rey
Phone: (310) 823-9647
Food: Pizza
Favorite Dish: Supreme Pizza

Hank's Pizza (Continued...)
Hours: Monday-Thursday,
Sunday 10 a.m.-10 p.m.,
Friday-Saturday 10 a.m.-11
p.m.
Accepts: Flexi-dollars only

**International House of
Pancakes**
Address: 2912 S. Sepulveda
Blvd., West Los Angeles
Phone: (310) 478-4017
Location: West Los Angeles
Food: American
Favorite Dish: Swedish
Pancakes, Cheeseburger and
Fries
Hours: 24 Hours
Accepts: Flexi-dollars only

Quizno's Subs
Address: 8321 Lincoln Blvd,
Los Angeles
Phone: (310) 641-6800
Location: Los Angeles
Food: Sandwiches and Salads
Favorite Dish:
Hours: Monday-Saturday 11
a.m.-9 p.m., Sunday 11 a.m.-8
p.m.
Accepts: Flexi-dollars only

Ruby's Diner
Address:13455 Maxella Ave.,
Marina del Rey
Phone: (310) 574-7829
Location: Marina del Rey
Food: American
Favorite Dish: Santa Fe Burger,
Aloha Burger, Peanut Butter
Cup Milkshake

Ruby's Diner (Continued....)

Hours: Sunday-Thursday 11 a.m.-9:30 p.m., Friday-Saturday 11 a.m.-10:30 p.m.

Accepts: Flexi-dollars only

Tower Pizza

Address: 8351 Lincoln Blvd., Los Angeles

Phone: (310) 410-4680

Location: Los Angeles

Food: Pizza

Favorite Dish: Pepperoni Pizza, Cheeseburger

24-Hour On-Campus Eating?

No

Student Favorites:

Jamba Juice

The Lion's Den

Did You Know?

LMU features special events like a **steak and lobster** dinner and a Valentine's Day dinner so that students can use up their LION dollars.

Funds for the meal plan are **non-transferable from one year to the next**, so use the money wisely.

Students can submit comments, suggestions, and recipes on a **bulletin board in the Lair**. Staff members respond in about a day, and often student suggestions influence the menu.

More places to use your LION dollars are on the way! Plans for an **on-campus convenience store and a pizza place** are in the works.

Other Options

Domino's Pizza delivers to on-campus locations, but students often choose to walk to nearby off-campus restaurants like Italy's Little Kitchen.

Students Speak Out On...
Campus Dining

"The food at the Lair is good, with the Grill and pizza being the high points. The Subway-style sandwich counter has a great meatball."

"It's not gourmet, but it's so much better than most schools. We have the snack shop and the cafeterias. We have two stands and another snack type shop in University Hall. Also special events such as the Valentine's Day dinner and Etiquette dinner have really good food. We also have a Jamba Juice. Yes, **there are good restaurants all around** that you can choose from. One is Little Italy's, which is really close and accepts Flexi. You can also buy a Domino's pizza delivery with Lion Dollars, but you can't put the tip on your lion dollars for some reason."

"Well, if you're a newcomer, the Lair will seem like option heaven, but **after awhile the food tastes the same,** and you never know what to decide between pasta, Mexican, burger, or sandwich. The Roski dining hall in University Hall is better, obviously, because all the teachers' offices are close by. Go to the Boar's Head for the best sandwiches ever! You have a nice view of the waterfall and the waterworks in the dining hall there."

"**The food quality isn't nearly as bad** as many people claim it to be."

"I am a vegetarian, and **there are almost no vegetarian options.** Even the veggie burgers are made with meat! And I don't even want to know what's in most of the food I eat there."

Q "It's okay. **Not good, but not bad**. I've definitely had better. Harvard College has better food! The Lion's Lair is the main place to eat, and the first freshman week it's pretty good, but it gets old very quickly because they serve the same choices every day. Only a few of the food "stands" are open late at night and on weekends, one of them being the junk food place, and I think it's terrible that just because you're there on weekends or can't get dinner late at night, you're left with basically junk food or bad sandwiches. I get so sad seeing so many people waiting at the junk food place!"

Q "Campus food is good until you have it more than fifty times. If there is only one criticism about the food is that it lacks variety, and I hear the menu changes like once every four years. The food is **made pretty well with the exception of the vegetables.** They are not fully cooked when they need to be."

Q "The dining hall is pretty spacious, but there is one area that is always blocked off for some reason. Still, **the dining hall is pretty spacious.** The most popular spots are Jamba Juice, The Lion's Den, and the coffee cart in between Seaver and Foley."

Q "The quality of the Lair food is great compared to what most schools have to put up with. **It's not home cooking,** but it's not that bad!"

Q "It's okay. **Some of the food tastes stale by Friday,** like the taco shells and the hamburger buns."

Q "Yuck. **It's so unhealthy to eat here**. I live on the salad bar and Jamba Juice because everything else is drowning in oil."

The College Prowler Take On...
Campus Dining

Walk into the dining hall on your first day of school, and The Lair is overwhelming. Pizza, pasta, burgers, burritos—where do you start? Is it possible to try everything The Lair offers in one school year? Unfortunately, the answer is yes. Although the food is appealing for the first few weeks, it quickly grows old. Occasionally, the menu changes slightly to accommodate student requests. The grill rotates new features each month—sometimes offering a Cajun burger or a bacon cheeseburger—but no matter what you call it, it is still the same burger. There are some highlights: The pasta is excellent, as are the Boar's Head sandwiches in Roski. Bread bowl soup every Wednesday and waffles are very popular. For vegetarians, the choices are limited to salad, pizza, or a veggie burger, although some campus vegetarians claim the veggie burger has meat in it. For students determined to eat healthy, food selection can be a frustrating process.

Finally, campus dining puts students in an interesting position. For students who opt out of the meal plan, the food is expensive, especially with added sales tax. Students with a meal plan often have money left over that is non-transferable; consequently, many students lose hundreds of dollars a year because they could not eat two thousand dollars worth of food. With or without a meal plan, you will pay significant amounts of money to eat on campus, and at the end of the year, the university may profit from your small appetite.

The College Prowler™ Grade on

Campus Dining: B-

Our grade on Campus Dining addresses the quality of both school-owned dining halls and independent on-campus restaurants as well as the price, availability, and variety of food.

Off-Campus Dining

The Lowdown On...
Off-Campus Dining

Restaurant Prowler:
Popular Places to Eat!

Baja Fresh Mexican Grill
Food: Mexican
Address: 13424 Maxella Ave., Marina del Rey
Phone: (310) 578-2252
Fax: (310) 574-8147
Price: $5 and up per person
Hours: Sunday-Monday 11 a.m.-9 p.m., Tuesday-Saturday 11 a.m.-10 p.m.

Bangkok West Thai
Food: Thai Fusion
Address: 606 Santa Monica Blvd., Santa Monica
Phone: (310) 395-9658
Fax: (310) 395-6567
Price: $10 per person
Hours: Monday-Friday 11 a.m.-3 p.m. and 5 p.m.-10 p.m., Saturday-Sunday 5 p.m.-10 p.m.

Bistro du Soliel
Food: French-American
Address: 6805 Vista del Mar, Playa del Rey

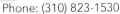

Phone: (310) 823-1530

Cool Features: This little bistro is in a converted house. Just look for the little yellow house on the corner of Vista del Mar and Culver Blvd. in Playa del Rey. The beach is around the corner.

Price: $9-$15 per person

Hours: Monday-Thursday 11 a.m.-2:30 p.m., 5 p.m.-9:30 p.m., Friday 9 a.m.-2:30 p.m. and 5 p.m.-10:30 p.m., Saturday 8 a.m.-10:30 p.m., Sunday 8 a.m.-9:30 p.m.

Buffalo Wings and Things

Food: American

Address: 11499 Jefferson Blvd., Culver City

Phone: (310) 477-3877

Fax: (310) 477-6023

Price: $5-$10 per person

Hours: Monday-Saturday 9 a.m.-11 p.m.

California Pizza Kitchen

Food: Gourmet Pizza

Address:13345 Fiji Way, Marina del Rey

Phone: (310) 301-1563

Fax: (310) 305-2843

Cool Features: A modern restaurant with a lot of variations on the plain old pizza.

Price: $8-$15 per person

Hours: Monday-Thursday 11 a.m.-10 p.m., Friday-Saturday 11 a.m.-11 p.m., Sunday 11:30 a.m.-10 p.m.

Cantalini's Salerno Beach Restaurant

Food: Italian

Address: 193 Culver Blvd., Playa del Rey

Phone: (310) 821-0018

Cool Features: A short walk to the beach

Price: $10-$15 per person

Hours: Closed on Monday, Tuesday-Friday 11:30 a.m.-10:30 p.m., Saturday-Sunday 4 p.m.-10:30 p.m.

The Cheesecake Factory

Food: American

Address: 4142 Via Marina, Marina del Rey

Phone: (310) 306-3344

Fax: (310) 827-8670

Cool Features: A huge menu with a long list of mixed drinks and desserts, valet parking for $2.75, heated patio overlooking the marina

Price: $10-$20 per person

Hours: Monday-Thursday 11:30 a.m.-11:30 p.m., Friday-Saturday 11:30 a.m.-12:30 a.m., Sunday 10 a.m.-11 p.m.

C&O Cucina

Food: Northern Italian

Address: 3016 Washington Blvd., Marina del Rey

Phone: (310) 301-7278

Cool Features: This tiny Italian restaurant features memorabilia of famous mobsters. Try the killer garlic

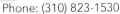

rolls! Delivery available.

Price: $10-$25 per person

Hours: Monday-Friday 11:30 a.m.-10 p.m. (Bar closes at 12 a.m.), Saturday-Sunday 11:30 a.m.-11 p.m. (Bar closes at 1:30 a.m.)

El Torito Mexican Restaurant and Cantina

Food: Mexican

Address: 13715 Fiji Way, Marina del Rey

Phone: (310) 823-8941

Fax: (310) 578-6921

Cool Features: For the over-21 crowd, El Torito features alcoholic beverages in wild colors. Also check out the Cadillac Margarita. Half-price appetizers on Monday 4 p.m.-10 p.m. in the Cantina.

Price: $8-$20

Hours: Monday-Friday 11 a.m.-10:30 p.m., Saturday-Sunday 11 a.m.-11 p.m.

Islands

Food: American

Address: 6081 Center Dr. Howard Hughes Center, Los Angeles

Phone: (310) 670-8580

Fax: (310) 670-8587

Cool Features: Hawaiian-themed restaurant featuring a variety of burgers. Be warned: fries must per purchased separately from meals.

Price: $8-$10

Hours: Monday-Friday 11:30 a.m.-11 p.m., Saturday-Sunday 11:30 a.m.-11:30 p.m

Italy's Little Kitchen

Address: 8516 Lincoln Blvd., Los Angeles

Phone: (310) 645-1220

Cool Features: This tiny Italian restaurant is a short walk from campus. Try the $9.95 pasta dishes on weekdays.

Price: $8-$15

Hours: Sunday-Thursday 11 a.m.-10:30 p.m., Friday-Saturday 11 a.m.-11:30 p.m.

Jerry's Famous Deli

Food: American

Address: 13181 Mindanao Way, Marina del Rey

Phone: (310) 821-6626

Price: $8-$15

Hours: 24 Hours a Day

Outlaws

Food: American

Address: 230 Culver Blvd., Playa del Rey

Phone: (310) 822-4040

Cool Features: This Western-themed restaurant features menu items named after famous outlaws (Annie Oakley, Pancho Villa, Richard Nixon.) To find Outlaws, look for the giant rock that forecasts the weather.

Price: $10 and up

Hours: Monday-Friday 11:30 a.m.-10 p.m., Saturday 9 a.m.-11 p.m., Sunday 9 a.m.-9 p.m.

Pick Up Stix

Food: Chinese-American Fast Food

Address: 1014 Wilshire Blvd., Santa Monica

Phone: (310) 395-4008

Fax: (310) 395-5070

Price: $5 and up

Hours: Sunday-Thursday 11 a.m.-9 p.m., Friday-Saturday 11 a.m.-9:30 p.m.

Ruby's Diner

Food: American

Address: 13455 Maxella Ave., Marina del Rey

Phone: (310) 574-7829

Fax: (310) 306-2186

Cool Features: 1950's theme, many flavors of milkshakes.

Price: $8 and up.

Hours: Sunday-Thursday 11 a.m.-9:30 p.m., Friday-Saturday 11 a.m.-10:30 p.m.

Sakura Japanese Restaurant

Food: Japanese

Address: 4545 Centinela Ave., Los Angeles

Phone: (310) 822-7790

Cool Features: Sushi Bar

Price: $10 and up

Hours: Closed on Monday, Tuesday-Friday 11:30 a.m.-2 p.m. and 5:30 p.m.-10 p.m., Saturday 5 p.m.-10 p.m., Sunday 5 p.m.-9:30 p.m.

The Shack

Food: American

Address: 185 Culver Blvd., Playa del Rey

Phone: (310) 823-6222

Price: $8-$15

Hours: Monday-Sunday 11 a.m.-10 p.m. (Bar closes at 2 a.m. Monday-Saturday and 10 p.m. Sunday.)

The Warehouse

Food: Seafood/American

Address: 4499 Admiralty Way, Marina del Rey

Phone: (310) 823-5451

Cool Features: Enter this Polynesian-themed restaurant by passing by the huge koi pond. An exterior patio overlooks the yachts in the marina. On some nights, a photographer will take your picture at the front entrance.

Fax: (310) 306-3952

Price: $12-$25

Hours: Saturday Brunch 11 a.m.-3 p.m., Sunday Brunch 10 a.m.-3 p.m., Monday-Friday Lunch 11:30 a.m.-3 p.m., Sunday-Thursday Dinner 5 p.m.-10 p.m., Friday-Saturday 5 p.m.-11 p.m.

Student Favorites:

Islands

Ruby's Diner

Chipotle

Italy's Little Kitchen

Late-Night Options:
Ruby's Diner
International House of
Pancakes
Jerry's Famous Deli

24-Hour Eating:
Jerry's Famous Deli

Closest Grocery Stores:
Albertson's
2627 Lincoln Blvd.
Los Angeles
Phone: (310) 452-3811

Albertson's
8448 Lincoln Blvd.
Westchester
Phone: (310) 645-3815

Ralph's
4700 Admiralty Way
Marina del Rey
Phone: (310) 823-4684

Ralph's
4311 Lincoln Blvd.
Marina del Rey
Phone: (310) 574-0909

Best Pizza:
California Pizza Kitchen

Best Mexican:
Chipotle

Best Seafood:
The Warehouse

Best Burgers:
Outlaws
Islands

Best Healthy:
Sakura Japanese Restaurant

Best Place to Take Your Parents:
The Cheesecake Factory
The Warehouse

Did You Know?

The Health Department grades Los Angeles County restaurants on an A, B, C, D, F scale. Most restaurants receive A's or B's, but watch out for restaurants with a rating of C or below.

Los Angeles offers literally any kind of food you could want. Within one mile of LMU, **you can grab Italian, Mexican, Thai, American, or pizza**. For more exotic fare, explore restaurants in Santa Monica or the city. You'll find a fusion of all different types of food.

Students Speak Out On...
Off-Campus Dining

> "There are so many restaurants all around, but students normally have so much money left on their Lion dollars that they should be eating at the school."

Q "One word: Chipotle! For Mexican, it's the best. Great chicken tacos. Pasta at Little Italy's Kitchen! I haven't been there, but I heard it's a decent place. **There is a Cheesecake Factory and an Olive Garden.** There are lots of places to go depending what type of food you fancy."

Q "The restaurants are good! There are everyone's favorite places like California Pizza Kitchen and IHOP, fast food places like KFC and Taco Bell, and many, many small ethnic places that have **absolutely excellent food.** Westchester/Marina is definitely the place to be if you like Mexican food, and there are also some excellent Asian places."

Q "The restaurants off campus are **extraordinarily good** and are a breather from the lack of variety that on-campus food provides. One of the most popular spots is Chipotle, which is really good. Another spot is Islands in the Howard Hughes Promenade, which is nearby LMU. Others include Italy's Little Kitchen, Cheesecake Factory, etc."

Q "There are tons of restaurants **from fast food to delivery to a nice sit-down meal!** Islands, IN-N-OUT Burger, etc."

Q "I hate campus food, so I always walk over to the restaurants on Lincoln. Italy's Little Kitchen is pretty good, and so is Tower Pizza. **It gets expensive if you do it too often,** but the food is good. Quizno's is good, too. If you have a car, you have access to more restaurants, including some really cool places on the marina."

Q "There are so many restaurants around here that you'll never get bored. Islands has the best burgers, and **if you're low-carbing, you can special order stuff.**"

Q "Great food everywhere. **There are a lot of places within walking distance of the campus,** but I always go into Marina del Rey. If you have a car, drive to Manhattan Beach for Chili's and Olive Garden. California Pizza Kitchen is also a must!"

Q "The marina has some good restaurants, but I hate spending over ten dollars for a meal. Restaurants at Howard Hughes or Third Street Promenade are cheaper. **Ruby's in the marina has great burgers**, and they take Flexi. I think Chipotle does, too."

The College Prowler Take On...
Off-Campus Dining

Off-campus dining is as diverse as Los Angeles. If you're in the mood for Italian, try southern Italian in Playa del Rey and northern Italian in the Marina. There are numerous pizza places within walking distance of campus, along with usual fast food staples like Quizno's, KFC, and Taco Bell. Venture away from campus, and you'll find restaurants appealing to all tastes and price ranges.

One popular locale for good food is Marina del Rey. Drive along Admiralty Way and drop in one of high-priced favorites that overlook the marina. Among the little seafood places is a franchise of The Cheesecake Factory; however, bring some cash because valet parking is mandatory. Another good option is The Warehouse. This Polynesian-themed restaurant offers steaks, lobster, and fish. If you want burgers, try Islands. There is no shortage of restaurants in the area. Try Venice, Playa del Rey, El Segundo, Manhattan Beach, and Santa Monica for more fine fare.

The College Prowler™ Grade on

Off-Campus Dining: A

A high off-campus dining grade implies that off-campus restaurants are affordable, accessible, and worth visiting. Other factors include the variety of cuisine and the availability of alternative options (vegetarian, vegan, Kosher, etc.).

On-Campus Housing

The Lowdown On...
On-Campus Housing

Best Dorms:
Doheny
Desmond
Rains
McCarthy
O'Malley

Worst Dorms:
Worst Dorms: Whelan
Rosecrans
Hannon

Dormitories

8000 House
Floors: 1
Total Occupancy: 7
Bathrooms: Shared
Co-Ed: Yes
Percentage of Men/Women: 57%/43%
Percentage of First-Year Students: 14% (1 of 7)
Room Types: 3 Double-Occupancy, 1 Single
Special Features: Front porch, back yard, living room,

8000 House (Continued....)

community room,

Location: Off-campus, at the corner of 80th Street and Loyola Blvd.

Theme: International House

8001 House

Floors: 1

Total Occupancy: 7

Bathrooms: Shared

Co-Ed: Yes

Percentage of Men/Women: 29%/71%

Percentage of First-Year Students: 0%

Room Types: 3 Double-Occupancy, 1 Single

Special Features: Front porch, back yard, living room, community room

Location: Off-campus, at the corner of 80th Street and Loyola Blvd.

Theme: Service and Action House

Desmond

Floors: 3

Total Occupancy: 170

Bathrooms: Shared per Floor

Co-Ed: No

Percentage of Men/Women: 0%/100%

Percentage of First-Year Students: 100%

Room Types: Traditional

Special Features: One sink per room

Doheny

Floors: 3

Total Occupancy: 117

Bathrooms: Shared per Floor

Co-Ed: Yes

Percentage of Men/Women: 39%/61%

Percentage of First-Year Students: 97%

Room Types: Traditional

Special Features: Sink in room, Elevator, Houses the First Year Institute Residential Program

Hannon Apartments

Floors: 2

Total Occupancy: 268

Bathrooms: In-room

Co-Ed: Yes

Percentage of Men/Women: 33%/67%

Percentage of First-Year Students: 7%

Room Types: One and two-bedroom apartments

Special Features: Furnished, appliances included, houses student workers

Huesman Hall

Floors: 1

Total Occupancy: 86

Bathrooms: Shared per Floor

Co-Ed: No

Percentage of Men/Women: 100%/0%

Percentage of First-Year Students: 100%

Room Types: Traditional

Special Features: Chapel, study rooms, community kitchen, access to Sullivan Lounge and Sullivan Academic Center

Leavey

Floors: 2

Total Occupancy: 56

Bathrooms: In-Room

Co-Ed: No

Percentage of Men/Women: 0%/100%

Percentage of First-Year Students: 75%

Room Types: Suite-style with common room

Special Features: Furnished common room, chapel, quiet rule

Leavey 4 Apartments

Floors: 4

Total Occupancy: 178

Bathrooms: In-Room

Co-Ed: Yes

Percentage of Men/Women: 46%/54%

Percentage of First-Year Students: 6%

Room Types: One and two-bedroom apartments

Special Features: Elevator, conference room, study room, full-size tub and shower, linen closet

Leavey 5 Apartments

Floors: 3

Total Occupancy: 174

Bathrooms: In-Room

Co-Ed: Yes

Percentage of Men/Women: 31%/69%

Percentage of First-Year Students: 3%

Room Types: One and two-bedroom apartments

Special Features: Full-size tub and shower, linen closet, elevator, study room

McCarthy

Floors: 4

Total Occupancy: 246

Bathrooms: In-room

Co-Ed: Yes

Percentage of Men/Women: 43%/57%

Percentage of First-Year Students: 8%

Room Types: Suite-style, Limited Private and Double Rooms

Special Features: Elevator, main lounge, 6 floor lounges, 6 study rooms, community kitchen, reading room, conference room, music practice room

McKay Hall

Floors: 4

Total Occupancy: 313

Bathrooms: In-Room

Co-Ed: Yes

Percentage of Men/Women: 21%/79%

Percentage of First-Year Students: 85%

Room Types: Suite-style

Special Features: Elevator, main lounge, 3 study rooms, snack shop

O'Malley Apartments

Floors: 4

Total Occupancy: 162

Bathrooms: In-Room

Co-Ed: Yes

Percentage of Men/Women: 22%/78%

Percentage of First-Year Students: 4%

Room Types: One, two, and three-bedroom apartments

Special Features: Elevator, linen closet, full-size tub and shower

Rains Hall

Floors: 3

Total Occupancy: 299

Bathrooms: In-Room

Co Ed: Yes

Percentage of Men/Women: 41%/59%

Percentage of First-Year Students: 7%

Room Types: Suite-style, Limited Private and Double Rooms

Special Features: Main lounge, 7 floor lounges, elevator, 7 study rooms, community kitchen, reading room, conference room, houses the Rains Intercultural Suite Experience (RISE)

Rosecrans

Floors: 3

Total Occupancy: 180

Bathrooms: Shared per Floor

Co-Ed: Yes

Percentage of Men/Women: 67%/33%

Percentage of First-Year Students: 98%

Room Types: Traditional

Special Features: Main lounge, 2 study rooms

Sullivan

Floors: 1

Total Occupancy: 85

Bathrooms: Shared per Floor

Co-Ed: No

Percentage of Men/Women: 0%/100%

Percentage of First-Year Students: 100%

Room Types: Traditional

Special Features: Main lounge, 2 study rooms, community kitchen, Academic Center

Tenderich Apartments

Floors: 3

Total Occupancy: 142

Bathrooms: In-Room

Co-Ed: Yes

Percentage of Men/Women: 46%/54%

Percentage of First-Year Students: 6%

Room Types: One and two-bedroom apartments

Special Features: Houses sophomore honors students, quiet rule

Whelan

Floors: 3

Total Occupancy: 180

Bathrooms: Shared per Floor

Co-Ed: Yes

Percentage of Men/Women: 67%/33%

Percentage of First-Year Students: 100%

Room Types: Traditional

Special Features: Main lounge, 2 study rooms

Undergrads on Campus:

48%

Number of Dormitories:

10

Number of University-Owned Apartments:

5

Bed Type:

Twin extra long. Can be arranged as bunk-beds, lofts, or captain's height

Also Available:

Special-interest housing

Quiet dorm

Summer housing

Available for Rent

Refrigerators through http://collegefridge.com

Cleaning Service?

Yes, but in public areas only approximately once a week.

You Get

Dorms include bed, desk with hutch and chair, dresser, wardrobe closet or built-in closet, mattress with mattress pad, bookcase, cable, HBO, Internet access. Apartments include, but are not limited to, sofas, tables, chairs, lamps, refrigerator, and stove/oven.

Room Types

- Dorm rooms include Traditional, Suite-style, and Suite-style with common room.

- Traditional—these rooms are double occupancy with a large common bathroom down the hall

- Suite-style—two double occupancy rooms share a small bathroom

- Suite-style with common room—two double occupancy rooms share a small bathroom. Six rooms share a common room.

- There are several on-campus apartment buildings that offer furnished one, two, and three-bedroom apartments, two students per bedroom. The apartments include a living room and kitchen.

- There are two off-campus theme houses that include bedrooms, living room, kitchen, bathrooms, and yard.

Did You Know?
More dorms are on the way! Leavey 6 Apartments and Loyola Hall should arrive soon! More apartments are in the planning phase, along with the convenience store and pizza place.

Microwaves, hot plates, and heating coils are not permitted in dorms. Halogen lamps are not permitted in campus housing.

"Avoid Whelan, Rosecrans, and the quad with those halls if you don't like rowdiness. Rains, McCarthy, and the Leaveys are nice because they're new. East Quad dorms are decent. McKay and Hannon are not so great."

"Nice, big, and spacious. **I love all the dorms**. If you're a girl, I'd say Desmond is the best bet because it's all girls, which is nice because guys can be loud. The rooms are also very spacious. Also, the fire alarm tends to be pulled in dorms that have boys. Rosecrans is ugly. All the apartments and suites look really cool."

"Dorms are what you'd expect. They get dirty; they're noisy since quiet rules are never enforced, and all the good stuff. But they're a vital part of the freshman experience, in my opinion. **You never get lonely** because it's so easy to go to the hall and find people to be with!"

"The dorm I lived in was co-ed in that guys lived on the first floor, and girls lived on the second and third floors which required keycard access. It was really fun, an**d I also felt safe knowing that you needed to swipe your keycard three times,** entering a secret code on the third time, in order to get into my room."

"The dorms are pretty good and decently equipped with a desk, bed, armoire, shelf, etc. **Many of the dorms are actually pretty to look at,** especially the more recently built dorms. The nicest dorms at LMU are McCarthy and Rains because they are new, so the architecture is exceptional. Sullivan is pretty good with it being one story, and the people there are extremely nice and pleasant to be around. The single sex dorms are not horrible or depriving in any sense. Moreover, they are better than the co-ed dorms."

"The dorms to avoid are McKay, Whelan and Rosecrans. The latter two because they are **notorious for being extremely wild and disorderly**, and there is this distinct odor, especially in Rosecrans. Also, these three dorms have been around for a long quite which is noticeable in the architecture."

"O'Malley is supposed to be beautiful. I lived in Leavey Center, which was an all girls, extremely quiet dorm with **some of the smallest rooms on campus.** It was nice, though, because it was a suite style with a huge common room for when you began to feel claustrophobic. All the dorms are nice by dorm standards, but it's what you make it. My best advice is to invest in a fridge."

"Desmond is a great dorm, and **I loved living there!"**

"**The chances for housing aren't great**. On the bright side, with the new Loyola Hall and Leavey 6 being built chances will be a lot better!"

"If you are a freshman or sophomore, your housing options are great. After that, well, good luck, because **LMU doesn't care where you live as long as they get their money."**

The College Prowler Take On...
On-Campus Housing

For your first two years at LMU, you have a variety of options for dorm life. Freshmen have many options. If you're into partying, try Whelan and Rosecrans, two of the older dorms. If you're more interested in some quiet time, try Sullivan or Huesman. Overall, though, every dorm has its fans, and students who obtain housing are happy with their new home. Newer apartments like O'Malley are beautiful and contrast significantly with the old, rundown look of Hannon and Tenderich. However, don't complain too much, because after sophomore year, you'll replace a crowded dorm with an expensive apartment. Housing is not guaranteed, or even likely, for upperclassmen, and right now, there is a major housing crisis. There is relief in sight. Two new dorms are under construction, scheduled to open for fall 2005. Until then, current sophomores, juniors, and seniors are stuck making off-campus arrangements.

Dorms are well-equipped with a reasonable amount of closet and drawer space. Students who are unhappy with sharing a bathroom with an entire floor can opt for one of the many suites on campus. Non-smoking and quiet dorms are available. Overall, the dorms offer students a variety of room types and buildings. The trick is getting a spot after your sophomore year.

B

The College Prowler™ Grade on

Campus Housing: B

A high Campus Housing grade indicates that dorms are clean, well-maintained, and spacious. Other determining factors include variety of dorms, proximity to classes, and social atmosphere.

Off-Campus Housing

The Lowdown On...
Off-Campus Housing

Undergrads in Off-Campus Housing:
52%

Best Time to Look for a Place:
April through June

Average Rent for a Studio Apartment:
$1000/month

Average Rent for a 1BR Apartment:
$1500/month

Average Rent for a 2BR Apartment:
$1800/month - $2100/month

Popular Areas:
Playa del Rey
Marina del Rey
Playa Vista

Student Housing Office:
Off-Campus Housing System
http://och.lmu.edu

Students Speak Out On...
Off-Campus Housing

"There's always roommate wanted ads around campus, so I don't think it's that hard to find. Besides, they are building two new dorms, and they are building expensive apartments all around the campus."

Q "Well, you're guaranteed housing if you had housing as a freshman, but **I don't think off-campus housing is worth it yet**. Maybe after sophomore or junior year you should consider off-campus housing."

Q "The good news: if you are a freshman that has lived on campus, you will get on-campus housing for your sophomore year, but it may not be your first choice dorm. When you are junior, you are not guaranteed on-campus housing. For the most part, there is always off-campus housing all over Westchester, Playa and Marina del Rey areas, which are minutes away from campus. **There is always availability for off-campus housing** because there is always an ad for someone in an off-campus apartment that needs a roommate for the year. Usually, the ads that float around have some lucrative deals for moving in."

Q "**Check newspapers, including The Loyolan**. Sometimes students post ads in the bathroom stalls, so that's always a good place to look. Even though they are building two new dorms, juniors and seniors need off-campus housing."

Q "Off-campus housing is a good idea, even for freshmen. You learn how to pay your own bills and survive on your own. **Get a roommate** and try one of the complexes in the Marina that many students use. It's expensive, but it's worth it."

Q "I moved into my own apartment halfway through freshman year, and I love it**. I live in a great apartment** with my own furniture, instead of crappy dorm furniture."

Q "I'm only a freshman, so I'm not worried about off-campus housing yet. **I've heard that many students live in Marina del Rey**, and Playa del Rey seems pretty cheap. There's always Westchester, but I don't think it's too popular."

Q "Marina del Rey is nice. If you're not from L.A., be prepared because apartments are expensive here. I have three roommates, and it still seems like a lot of money for such a small place. **We have an ocean view,** which is cool."

Q **"LMU doesn't provide enough housing**, so get ready to live off campus. It's okay, I guess, because everyone leaves campus on the weekends anyway. When I lived on campus, it got really boring on weekends because everyone goes home."

Q "Get a car, and move off campus. **It's the only way to live."**

Q "I live at home and commute. Considering tuition is so expensive and financial aid sucks, I need all of the money I can get. **Living at home is really the only option for me."**

The College Prowler Take On...
Off-Campus Housing

Most students at LMU tire of campus housing by sophomore year, and beyond sophomore year, it is nearly impossible to get a spot in student housing. Consequently, an off-campus apartment is inevitable for all but a few students, so it is a good idea to learn the area. Popular locations include Marina del Rey and its sister city, Playa del Rey. Marina del Rey is home to tons of apartment complexes, including the pricey Water Terrace to the mid-range places like Chateau Marina, The Bay Club, and Marina Pointe. If you want a bigger space for less money, look into buildings in Playa del Rey. This small beach-town houses smaller apartment buildings of several units and a few major complexes like Archstone. The major plus of Playa del Rey is the beach; most apartments are within walking distance or a several minute drive. The downside to Playa is that no major freeways hook up with the town, so you have to go through Marina del Rey or Culver City to access Los Angeles. In spite of its lack of freeway access, traffic is still heavy during rush hour.

LMU overlooks the planned community of Playa Vista, a rapidly expanding area that contains apartment buildings and condos, with many more on the way. This is an area to watch because a shopping center is also in the works. Prices at the apartments fall between Marina del Rey on the more expensive side and Playa del Rey on the cheaper end. Playa Vista is also closest to LMU.

B+

The College Prowler™ Grade on
Off-Campus
Housing: A

A high grade in Off-Campus Housing indicates that apartments are of high quality, close to campus, affordable, and easy to secure.

Diversity

The Lowdown On...
Diversity

American Indian:
1%

Asian or Pacific Islander:
13%

African American:
9%

Hispanic:
17%

White:
58%

International:
1%

Unknown:
1%

Out-of-State:
28%

Political Activity

Even though the school is Roman Catholic, the Jesuit mission of promoting social justice attracts many liberals. Most students are politically active, and both College Republicans and Young Democrats are visible presences. It is not unusual to see protests and memorials on campus, sponsored by the Center for Service and Action. Amnesty International and the Human Rights Coalition have a presence on campus. Whether you're liberal, conservative, independent, or just apathetic, the school promotes participation in the political system with activities like voter registration, speakers, and protests.

Service Organization

LMU involves students in unique service projects all over the world. Students can opt to spend spring break in a third-world country, and De Colores, a student organization that builds houses for the poor in Mexico, is extremely popular and active. Other organizations like Belles and Ignatians are so popular that competition to get in is fierce.

Gay Tolerance

While there is no active anti-gay sentiment on campus, this is a Catholic institution, and therefore, there are certainly a number of people on campus who are not entirely accepting of sexualities other than heterosexual. There are, however, a couple organizations on campus working to improve people's attitudes regarding the GLBT community on campus.

Most Popular Religions

Most students are Roman Catholic and hail from parochial schools. However, the school supports other religions and cultures. There is a strong Jewish community on campus that hosts celebrations for Passover and other religious holidays. Also, there is a significant Muslim population, but there is no active organization. The Christian Life Community (CLC) is extremely active on campus and offers students religious, academic, and social support. Students view them as one big, happy family.

Economic Status

There is a wide gulf between the "haves" and "have nots" on campus. Many students come from wealthy families, so expensive cars and clothes are the rule rather than the exception. However, for every new Mercedes in the parking lot, there are a few Toyotas. There does seem to be some tension between the upper and middle classes.

Minority Clubs

The students are a diverse bunch. Whatever your ethnicity or culture, there is an organization for you. De Colores, Black Student Union, and professional groups like Chicanos for Creative Medicine draw a lot of students.

Students Speak Out On...
Diversity

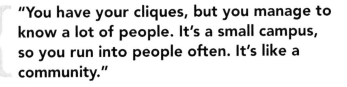

"You have your cliques, but you manage to know a lot of people. It's a small campus, so you run into people often. It's like a community."

Q "Some people think it's diverse. I'm sorry, but it's not. Most people are Catholic, which should be expected in a Catholic school. There are many blonde American types. Pretty WASP, minus the Protestant. There are a couple Asians and African Americans and Latinos, but not that many compared to what LA is really like. I'd have to say **it's diverse to some people not from LA,** but for LA natives, it's not diverse at all."

Q "Very diverse. At first sight at the preview day, **it seemed predominantly Caucasian,** but my assumptions were proven wrong. Among the larger minorities are African Americans, Latinos, and Hawaiians."

Q "Personally, **I don't think this campus is diverse at all.** I feel like 80% of the student body is white even though the stats say about 55%-60%. Every time I walk around campus, I don't see many minorities. I see more whites than anything else. Furthermore, I feel like I am seeing the same people, terms of ethnicity, over and over again. The next largest minority group is Latinos at 20%."

Q "Diversity is an important thing for me. I want to see different ethnicities and groups. Interestingly enough, the freshmen class is pretty diverse, coming from forty different states. It's pretty extraordinary to think that someone from Texas heard of LMU and decided to attend. As far as locations, it is pretty diverse, but **as far as ethnicity, not even close.** There is still a lot of work ahead to attain that type of diversity at LMU."

Q "The campus is very diverse. **There is a club for every race, color, shape, size and sexual orientation** you could imagine."

Q "LMU strives to keep a diverse campus, and I believe that through certain programs and events, such as the Bellarmine Forum, they are very successful. However, **there is never too little diversity!"**

Q "It seems pretty diverse to me. **You have your share of blonde Abercrombie models,** but you also have a ton of people who are from different backgrounds."

Q "Racially, I think the campus is diverse, but economically, we're not. **Everybody comes from the same upper middle-class background**. The school doesn't seem to do much to get families with less money here even though they claim that we're so diverse."

Q "There are a lot of mixed-race people here, so **I don't feel like I'm in the minority."**

Q "Diverse? Not here. **Everybody is blonde and wealthy."**

The College Prowler Take On...
Diversity

The LMU community encompasses students from many states and countries. There are large Filipino and Hawaiian populations, along with a significant number of Latinos and African-Americans. More importantly, these groups are very vocal in campus affairs. Each group has one or more clubs to represent its unique culture, interests, and history. Additionally, many clubs seek to unite the various ethnicities and establish dialogues. Groups like the Middle Eastern Club, De Colores, Soul Food, and others welcome all students into their memberships.

The university administration prides themselves on creating this diverse, open campus. However, students disagree on whether or not the university is as diverse as the administration claims. The numbers show that Caucasians are still a strong majority on campus with 58% represented, while other ethnicities have less than 20% total. Many students feel that these numbers accurately reflect the racial breakdown of the campus. Regardless of the percentages, LMU offers students of every race, culture, and ethnicity a community on campus. The students, not the university, deserve the credit for improving the diversity on campus.

B+

The College Prowler™ Grade on

Diversity: B+

A high grade in Diversity indicates that ethnic minorities and international students have a notable presence on campus and that students of different economic backgrounds, religious beliefs, and sexual preferences are well-represented.

Guys & Girls

The Lowdown On...
Guys & Girls

Men Undergrads:
40%

Women Undergrads:
60%

Birth Control Available?
Yes, birth control is available from the health center.

Social Scene
After one semester, students know almost everyone on campus because everyone is very outgoing. Everyone interacts in class and out. Orientation is a big ice-breaker, and the dorms allow for close interaction and strong friendships. Students tend to hang out with other students within their majors, so seeking out students with similar majors and interests is a must. There are some cliques among students in film, biology, and engineering.

Hookups or Relationships?

Many students are in serious relationships, and by sophomore year, many couples share an off-campus apartment. Students looking for random hookups will always find someone looking for that level of commitment. The guys on campus seem more interested in just hooking up, while many of the girls are after Mr. Right.

Best Place to Meet Guys/Girls:

Dorms, extracurricular activities, and yes, classes are the most popular ways to meet the opposite sex. The Rec Center is a popular place before and after class, so check out the pool and the gym. Students often meet their perfect match by joining the same club, CLC group, or service organization.

Dress Code

If it's in style, chances are LMU students are wearing it. Most students look like they stepped out of an Abercrombie and Fitch catalogue, while Armani Exchange, Diesel, and Juicy Couture also rule. Bring your UGG boots and flip-flops, because few students just roll out of bed and go to class in their pajamas.

Did You Know?

Top Places to Find Hotties:
- Dorms
- Gym
- Sororities/Frats

Top Places to Hookup:
- Off-campus parties
- Dorms
- Empty classrooms
- Bus parties
- Clubs

Students Speak Out On...
Guys & Girls

"I'd say that there are no especially ugly people at LMU. Everyone is very presentable, though. Hey, this is LA where everyone is in the latest fashions, and everyone tries to look their best."

Q **"Girls outnumber guys**, so it's kind of hard to find that one guy because he might be taken."

Q "Our school has an obvious female majority, but there's definitely nothing negative in that! The guys/girls are as diverse as they would be at any school, in everything from ethnicity to interests, so it's not so easy to generalize. One thing I can say is that this school is definitely a "beach" school—girls go out to the dorm courtyards in bikinis and guys go out shirtless in order to get tans, and "beach" fashion, meaning **flip-flops, tans, bleached hair, a large flower on your ear,** is very popular here. We also have a huge Hawaiian population, which adds to the laid-back, feel-good beach atmosphere."

Q "From what I have seen and noticed, **the guys are pretty shy**. I don't know why that would be the case, maybe it is just the freshmen. The guys are pretty much in the middle ground: They are not too smart or too stupid or too arrogant or passive. Surprisingly, many of the guys I have encountered or talked to have been extremely nice and cordial many times. Of course, for the most part, the guys are pretty attractive."

Q "There are a lot more girls on campus than guys, and for some reason **the hot guys are in hibernation until second semester.** Then, they are worth the wait: hot and relatively intelligent. It's a nice thing. What isn't nice is that the girls are just as hot, and the competition is tight."

Q "Everyone is really nice and pleasant to get along with— guys and girls alike. **There is always someone ready to talk with you** about anything on your mind!"

Q "There aren't enough guys here, which sucks for us girls. Yeah, **everybody's hot,** but that only matters if that is the only thing you base your relationships on."

Q "Students are nice, and this is L.A., so of course **everybody is nice to look at.**"

The College Prowler Take On...
Guys & Girls

LMU students reflect L.A.'s obsession with appearance. Everyone here looks good and dresses well. The general attitude of students is that the student body is hot. While that may seem intimidating to some, students are mostly friendly and outgoing. After the frenzy of the first semester of the school year, by the time students return from winter break, they are more relaxed and social.

The ratio of guys to girls on campus means that when finding members of the opposite sex, the guys have a greater advantage. LMU girls typically look outside of the school for a guy, and Los Angeles' other colleges are good places to begin. Even though LMU is a Catholic school, students are not strangers to sex. Although stories of girls sleeping with entire fraternities are rare, many students are in serious, committed relationships. However, if you just want to have fun, chances are you can find someone here after the same thing.

The College Prowler™ Grade on Guys: A

A high grade for Guys indicates that the male population on campus is attractive, smart, friendly, and engaging, and that the school has a decent ratio of guys to girls.

The College Prowler™ Grade on Girls: A+

A high grade for Girls not only implies that the women on campus are attractive, smart, friendly, and engaging, but also that there is a fair ratio of girls to guys.

Athletics

The Lowdown On...
Athletics

Athletic Division:
NCAA Division I

Conference:
West Coast Conference
Pacific Collegiate Swimming Conference
Western Water Polo Association
Western Athletic Conference
Western Intercollegiate Rowing Association

Intercollegiate Varsity Sports

Men's Teams:
Baseball
Basketball
Crew
Cross Country
Golf
Soccer
Tennis
Water Polo

Women's Teams:
Basketball
Crew
Cross Country
Soccer
Softball
Swimming
Tennis
Volleyball
Water Polo

Club Sports:
Rugby
Men's Lacrosse
Women's Lacrosse
Men's Volleyball
Men's Club Soccer
Fencing
Women's Volleyball
Scuba

Intramurals:
Basketball
Outdoor Soccer
Table Tennis
Foosball
6 on 6 Volleyball
Ultimate Frisbee
Innertube Waterpolo

Fields:
Page Stadium
Sullivan Field
LMU Outdoor Complex

School Mascot:
Lion

Getting Tickets

For students, faculty, and staff, admission is free. For guests, tickets vary in price per sport. They range from four to eight dollars, while season tickets are more expensive, sometimes several hundred dollars. For tickets, go to the ticket office across from the entrance to Gersten Pavilion or call (310) 338-6095. Credit cards are accepted over the phone.

Most Popular Sport

Women's sports rule at LMU. Women's volleyball and basketball are popular. Men's sports like baseball, basketball, and lacrosse have their own following. Generally, sports have a small, loyal fan base, but overall, LMU athletics do not receive the attention that they deserve.

Overlooked Teams

While basketball and baseball receive the most attention, other sports at LMU are neglected until a particular team has a fabulous season. Students hear almost nothing about tennis, soccer, and cross-country. Water polo is gaining in popularity because LMU boasts a particularly good team.

Best Place to Take a Walk

LMU does not boast any walking trails, but students interested in a hike should check out trails in Malibu. There is also a bike path that links Marina del Rey and Playa del Rey. The best place for a walk in the immediate area is the beach in Playa del Rey.

Gyms/Facilities

Burns Recreation and Aquatics Center

Burns Rec Center houses the university's pool and gym. The gym boasts a huge collection of free weights, machines, and other exercise equipment. Burns also contains classrooms for aerobics, Pilates, and yoga classes. Two basketball courts allow for a casual game, while non-athletes can hang out and play table tennis or swim in the pool. Two locker rooms provide lockers and showers for students. Although the gym does get crowded in the afternoon, there is plenty of room for students to work out. A wait for equipment is rare.

George C. Page Stadium

Home to LMU baseball, Page stadium features a classic look with a manual scoreboard. It also features the Lion's Mikos Blue Monster, a 130-foot wide and 37-foot tall replica of Fenway Park's Green Monster. The stadium seats more than 600 people with VIP seating for 200.

Gersten Pavilion

Adjacent to Burns Rec Center is Gersten Pavilion, which was built for the 1984 Olympics in Los Angeles. Gersten hosts indoor sports like basketball and volleyball. The arena also has a memorable history. The men's basketball team posted a sixteen-game winning streak in 1987 and 1988. Currently, the pavilion also is home to LMU's winning women's volleyball team.

LMU Boathouse

This facility on the marina in Marina del Rey opened in 2002. It includes two boat bays, a work area, an office, a new dock, and restrooms.

LMU Outdoor Complex

This complex features the softball field and tennis courts. Recently renovated, the softball field is now ranked among the top playing surfaces in the Pacific Coast Softball Conference. Additionally, the tennis courts received a new look and now sport the school's colors of crimson and navy blue. A sixth court is under construction.

Sullivan Field

LMU boasts one of the top soccer fields in the West Coast Conference, thanks to the beautiful Sullivan Field. Sweden, Italy, and Argentina used Sullivan during the 1994 FIFA World Cup, and in 1998, teams in the Gold Cup Tournament used Sullivan as a practice field. Beginning in 2002, Sullivan became the practice site for the Rose Bowl; consequently, the field received new turf.

Students Speak Out On...
Athletics

"Well, I haven't been to any kind of game. There have been many successes with some teams, so it's not too bad. I guess if you have time I heard it's good to relax and show some support."

Q "I don't think sports are that huge. I wish they were, though, because that would bring more boys. We don't have a football team, which is a big downer. The school wanted to be small, so **they got rid of the football field.** Our biggest sport is basketball, and I don't think we're that good. Our rival is Pepperdine. I say we forget the small school crap and build us a football and track field before it's too late!"

Q "Intercollegiate sports are not as big here. **The most popular sport at LMU is basketball,** and even then, it is not a big deal. Ever since the departure of football at LMU and failure at several attempts after 1988 to get to the NCAA tournament in basketball, sports have not been really at the center in LMU. IM sports are not as big either. Sometimes, I feel that when Campus Recreation promotes IM sports, it is like they are desperate for people, and their main targets are the freshmen class because they know no one else will play."

Q "Each sport has its own crowd of devoted fans, but **sports are not an overwhelming presence on campus**. Intramural sports are fun if you can get people to stay committed to going."

Q "Neither varsity or IM sports seemed to be too important, even though they were publicized and held. **More support seems to be needed!"**

Q "Volleyball is pretty big here, but **I haven't been to any games."**

Q "The games are **great if you have time.** Our basketball team used to be really good."

Q **"Lady Lions basketball rocks!** They won the conference, and they played in New Mexico against Baylor."

Q "If you have not seen the volleyball team, go check 'em out! **Our team was amazing this year."**

The College Prowler Take On...
Athletics

Unlike other large schools in the area, like USC and UCLA, LMU lacks a football team. Perhaps this is the reason that the student body does not rally around sports teams. Students interested in sports go to USC, while students interested in the arts go to LMU. Athletics are huge among the athletes, but the ordinary student body is generally apathetic to the school's sports teams. It's too bad because the women's teams at LMU are really talented. Both the women's volleyball and women's basketball teams are among the top teams in the nation. Among the guys, men's lacrosse receives some attention from students. Although the school does offer IM sports, the challenge is to get students to participate and stick with them.

LMU is not a major sports school, but the teams deserve more support. For female athletes, LMU offers a chance to play at a school where the women's teams have a stronger fan base than the men. The school offers women a strong athletic program in basketball, volleyball, swimming, water polo, and more. However, LMU needs to build more support overall for both men and women.

The College Prowler™ Grade on
Athletics: B

A high grade in Athletics indicates that students have school spirit, that sports programs are respected, that games are well-attended, and that intramurals are a prominent part of student life.

Nightlife

The Lowdown On...
Nightlife

Club and Bar Prowler: Popular Nightlife Spots!

Clubs:

A.D.

836 N. Highland Ave.,
Los Angeles (near Melrose)

(323) 467-3000

This elegant, medieval-themed club is both friendly to both straights and gays. Cocktail waitresses look like Britney Spears in schoolgirl uniforms.

Keep your eyes peeled for Drew Barrymore, Janet Jackson, and Mark Wahlberg. Valet and street parking.

Hours: Friday-Saturday 10 p.m.-2 a.m.

Saturday: "Social Studies Night." More mellow than the typical rave scene.

Avalon

1735 Vine St., Hollywood

(323) 462-3000

Formerly known as the Hollywood Palace, Avalon is one of L.A.'s megaclubs and features a café, lobby, balcony,

Avalon (Continued....)

lounge, and VIP Spider Room. This prestigious club features DJ nights and some top bands. Events and prices vary. Parking is $15 for self-parking. Valet is also available.

Circle Bar

2926 Main St., Santa Monica

(310) 450-0508

One of the hottest and trendiest nightclubs in Santa Monica. Circle Bar is not low-key; the dance floor is typically packed with drunk college kids over twenty-one. It's crowded, so there may be a wait to get in. No cover charge to get in.

Hours: 8:30 p.m.-2 a.m.

Circus Disco

6655 Santa Monica Blvd., Los Angeles

(323) 462-1291

L.A. hotspot with a cost of anywhere from $3-$25. Both valet and street parking are available.

Club Lingerie

6507 Sunset Blvd., Hollywood

(323) 466-8557

This legendary Hollywood club features live bands and dancing. Some nights feature ska, rock, and electronica. Two levels feature bars and VIP lounges that require "industry connections" to get in. Valet parking available. Do not park at the Jack in the Box, or you will get towed. Cover varies.

Hours: 9 p.m.-2 a.m.

Club 7969

7969 Santa Monica Blvd, Los Angeles

(323) 654-0280

Dragonfly

6510 Santa Monica Blvd., Los Angeles

(323) 466-3416

http://www.dragonfly.com

Dragonfly is definitely unique. It features an eclectic mix of rock and reggae, live music, and dancing. Valet and street parking. Cover varies.

Hours: 9 p.m.-2 a.m.

El Centro

6202 Santa Monica Blvd, Los Angeles

Covered in black paint and bearing no sign, El Centro is a unique spot in a shady area of Hollywood. Thursday is the choice night for celebs like Kelly Osbourne to pop in, but if you don't have the right connections, it is nearly impossible to get in. Tuesday is more laid-back. Monday and Tuesday nights are free. On Thursday nights, unless you show up with Paris Hilton, bring your wallet to bribe the doorman.

Hours: Monday-Tuesday, Thursday 10 p.m.-2 a.m.

El Cid

4212 Sunset Blvd., Silver Lake

(323) 668-0318

http://rockula.com/elcid.html

El Cid features live DJs, alternative bands, brunch fashion shows, and salsa music. Grab a booth at El Cid, and may spot Jack Black. Street parking and a free lot. $27 cover on flamenco night.

Hours: Monday-Tuesday 9 p.m.-2 a.m., Wednesday-Sunday 6 p.m.-2 a.m.

El Dorado

11777 San Vicente Blvd., Los Angeles

(310) 207-0150

http://www.eldoradocantina.com

At El Dorado, you'll find a Mexican menu with a party atmosphere. Valet and metered street parking.

Tuesday: "Tamale Tuesday." $1 tacos, $2 tamales, and cheap Tecates

Thursday: Check out tarot card readers, go-go dancers, and prizes. Call ahead.

Hours: Monday 12 p.m.-12 a.m., Tuesday-Saturday 12 p.m.-2 a.m.

Forbidden City

1718 Vine St., Hollywood (at Hollywood Blvd.)

(323) 461-2300

Forbidden City features Asian décor with a moderately-priced Chinese menu. The club features a lounge, open-air patios, and a VIP area. There is no cover chargebut you will have wait in line. Metered street parking available.

Hours: Everyday 6 p.m.-2 a.m.

Gabah

4658 Melrose Ave., Los Angeles

(323) 664-8913

Gabah is a mellower hip-hop club in East Hollywood. Watch out for an unannounced visit from Black-Eyes Peas.

Hours: Erratic. Arrive after 10:30 p.m.

Gotham Hall

1431 Third St., Santa Monica

(310) 394-8865

Situated on the Third Street Promenade, Gotham Hall is huge and can satisfy any craving. It features a restaurant with pool tables and large screen TVs, club, and dance floors. DJs spin hip-hop, house, and reggae. Arrive before 9:30 p.m. for free drinks in the main bar and free admission. Lot parking is available, and the cover charge varies.

Hours: 5 p.m.-11 p.m.

Ivar

6356 Hollywood Blvd., Hollywood

(323) 465-4827

There is always a line to enter this industrial club in Hollywood. The décor is edgy, softened somewhat by orange vinyl couches. Guys buy tables, or "pods," to attract younger patrons with drinks. Tables require a two-bottle minimum at $250 a bottle. DJs and live bands play a variety of music. $20 cover charge and valet parking.

Hours: Wednesday-Saturday 9:30 p.m.-4 a.m.

Jewel's Catch One

4067 W. Pico Blvd., Los Angeles

(323) 734-8849

http://www.jewelscatchone. com

The Catch features salsa, hip-hop, and house for a mostly lesbian crowd. Madonna threw her launch party for "Music" here. Free parking in the club lot.

Friday and Sunday: Drink specials from 5 p.m.-9 p.m.

Hours: Wednesday-Saturday 9 p.m.-2 a.m., Sunday 9 p.m.-2 a.m.

Sunday: 18 and up night.

Joseph's Café

1775 Ivar Ave., Hollywood

(323) 462-8697

Populated by actors, models, and pop-stars, including Britney Spears, Jospeh's has been around since the 40's and still holds its charm. Be prepared to wait in line unless you show up with Britney herself. Valet and street parking available. $10-$15 cover charge.

Monday: Manic Mondays

Friday: Hip-hop party

Saturday: "Siren"

Hours: Monday-Tuesday 10 p.m.-2 a.m., Friday-Saturday 10 p.m.-2 a.m.

King King

6555 Hollywood Blvd., Los Angeles

(323) 960-9234

This large loft space features red brick walls, exposed ceiling, and velvet curtains. A large bar sits in the center of the club along with low sofas. King King features live music, DJs, and dancing. Parking is free, and the cover runs from $5-$10.

Hours: Monday-Thursday 9 p.m.-2 a.m.

Friday-Saturday 9 p.m.- 4 a.m.

Level 3

Hollywood and Highland Complex

(323) 461-2017

Formerly the underage club One Seven, Level 3 is all grown up. The club features a real bar, beds, and a sophisticated menu. Level 3 features DJs and live bands playing hip-hop and house. Under twenty-one? Check out KIIS FM's Club DV8 on Saturdays. Parking is available in the underground garage. The cover is $10-$20.

Wednesday: Live acts

Friday: DJs

Saturday: Over-18 dance party sponsored by KIIS FM.

Hours: Monday, Wednesday, Friday, Saturday 10 p.m.-2 a.m.

Prey

643 N. La Cienega Blvd., Los Angeles

(310) 652-2012

Slick club featuring top promoters. Thursdays are Club Twist, and Saturdays are Club Prey. Parking is valet, and the cover is $10-$20 unless you are on the guest list.

QC2020

901 Via San Clemente, Montebello

(323) 724-4500

This state-of-the-art dance club channels Vegas with two dance floors, plasma screens, and a glass bottom go-go cage. Arrive early on most nights,

QC2020 (Continued....)

and they'll waive the cover. QC2020 features a secure parking lot.

Wednesday-Sunday: $2 well drinks, casual dress code, free buffet.

Shelter

8117 Sunset Blvd., West Hollywood

(323) 654-0030

Shelter is a trendy club that reinvents itself every few months to keep up with the L.A. club scene. There is typically a long line unless you show up for dinner at 8 p.m. Club doors open at 9:30 p.m.

Hours: Thursday-Saturday 8 p.m.-2 a.m.

Sugar

814 Broadway, Santa Monica (at Lincoln)

(310) 899-1989

This sleek club in Santa Monica features electronic music and a celestial décor. Different nights feature different styles. Thursdays feature exotic genres like Arab electronica, Aboriginal dub, and Afrotech. Can't find Sugar? There's no sign, but it's right next door to Swingers. Valet, lot, and street parking are all available.

Hours: Thursday-Saturday 10 p.m.-2 a.m.

The Space

2020 Wilshire Blvd.,
Santa Monica

(310) 829-1933

Formerly Lush, The Space features Top 40 hits and 1980's music. Friday features the band Fast Times, while Saturdays feature current pop like Britney. The parking is valet, but the covers are cheap: $5 on Fridays and $5-$10 on Saturdays.

Hours: Friday-Saturday 8 p.m.-2 a.m.

The Viper Room

8852 Sunset Blvd.,
West Hollywood

(310) 358-1880

The Viper Room is still legendary in Hollywood. River Phoenix overdosed here, and Tommy Lee assaulted a photographer. Johnny Cash, Courtney Love, and Lenny Kravitz played a set in The Viper Room, and more stars show up. If you're over 21, this place should be on your list for its history alone.

Hours: 9 p.m.-2 a.m.

Zanzibar

1301 5th St., Santa Monica

(310) 451-2221

http://www.zanzibarlive.com

This Moroccan-themed club features Los Angeles DJs spinning electronica. Zanzibar features a wraparound bar and a list of DJs worth checking

Zanzibar (Continued....)

out for those twenty-one and over. Arrive early to beat the long line. Cover varies, and payment is cash only.

Hours: Wednesday-Sunday 9 p.m.-2 a.m.

Bars:

Alibi Room

12236 W. Washington Blvd.,
Los Angeles

(310) 398-5516

Looking for a low-key night out? Check out this Culver City dive. Within its faux wood walls, locals drink cheap beer and play pool. There's no cover, and parking is on the street.

Hours: 10 p.m.-2 a.m.

Busby's

3110 Santa Monica Blvd.,
Santa Monica

(310) 828-4567

This sports bar pleases a wide range of patrons. Happy hour brings in local businessmen for free snacks and discounted drinks, but after 9 p.m., surfers and college students pour in for the hip-hop and house music. There are also free pool tables and backgammon. There is a $10 cover charge on Thursday-Saturday.

Monday-Friday: Happy Hour features a free buffet and $1 off drinks. There are also 4 p.m.-7 p.m. drink specials. Hours: 10 a.m.-2 a.m.

Cameo Bar at Viceroy Hotel

1819 Ocean Ave.,
Santa Monica

(310) 451-8711

Cameo Bar is not your typical beachside bar. This bar is definitely more luxurious and expensive. It features a full menu, swimming pool, and outdoor lounge. There is a charge for valet parking.

Hours: 11 a.m.-2 a.m.

Chez Jay's

1657 Ocean Ave.,
Santa Monica

(310) 395-1741

Locals favor this beachside bar's nautical theme, complete with mounted fish. Celebs like Frank Sinatra and Marlon Brando once frequented Jay's, but now you're more likely to spot George Clooney. Less upscale than Cameo Bar up the street, Chez Jay's appeal is in the relaxed atmosphere.

Hours: Monday-Friday 12 p.m.-2 p.m. and 6 p.m.-2 a.m., Saturday-Sunday 9 a.m.-1:45 p.m. and 6 p.m.-2 a.m.

Good Hurt

12249 Venice Blvd.,
Los Angeles

(310) 390-1076

Only in L.A. will you find a bar based entirely on a medical theme. Waitresses dressed up like nurses serve drinks called Black and Blue or Transfusion. Although the bar features first-aid kits for decoration, it

Good Hurt (Continued....)

lacks the bright lights of an emergency room.

Hours: Monday-Saturday 8 p.m.-2 a.m.

Lounge 217

217 Broadway, Santa Monica

(310) 394-6336

Close to the Third Street Promenade, Lounge 217 features dancing and drinks. The cover is expensive, but it is possible to get into the VIP lounge.

Hours: Wednesday-Saturday 9 p.m.-2 a.m.

Rusty's Surf Ranch

256 Santa Monica Pier,
Santa Monica

(310) 393-7386

Ocean Avenue too upscale? Check out Rusty's on Santa Monica Pier, but watch out for the tourists. Rusty's features a full menu, live music, and karaoke. Parking is $8.

Hours: Monday-Friday 4 p.m.-2 a.m., Saturday-Sunday 12 p.m.-2 a.m.

Shane

2424 Main St., Santa Monica

(310) 396-4122

This bar features dinner until 11 p.m., and then the crew pushes the tables aside for the dance floor. After that, Shane evolves into a hip-hop club. There is a large covered patio

Shane (Continued....)

for smokers. Overall, Shane is crowded and noisy.

Hours: Tuesday-Wednesday 5 p.m.-10 p.m., Thursday-Saturday 5 p.m.-1 a.m., Sunday 11 a.m.-4 p.m.

Temple Bar

1026 Wilshire Blvd., Santa Monica

(310) 393-6611

A variety of live music is the first reason to hit Temple Bar. The Asian-themed décor mix with live world music, hip-hop, or billiards. The bar is for twenty-one and over, and the cover varies.

Hours: 7 p.m.-2 a.m.

The Jazz Bakery

3233 Helms Ave., Culver City

(323) 271-9039

This unique spot aims to provide fabulous jazz to a wide audience, and it succeeds. The small space seats 230 with a stage that can hold a big band or lone performer. There is a menu, but the music alone is what makes The Jazz Bakery special.

Every night: Half-price rush tickets every night for students with a valid ID.

Hours: Monday-Friday 8 p.m. and 9:30 p.m. shows, Sunday 4:30 p.m. matinees.

Other Places to Check Out:

ACME Comedy Theatre

135 N. La Brea Ave., Los Angeles (323) 525-0202

This first-rate comedy club features talented performers, improve, and sketch comedy. Look for it between W. 1st St. and Beverly Blvd.

The Comedy Store

8433 W. Sunset Blvd., West Hollywood

(323) 656-6225

Three stages feature a variety of comedians from big names to rookies. The Main Room at $20 per show features the biggest comics, while the Original Room has daily shows. There is also the Belly Room, and the occasional karaoke night. The cost is usually a two-drink minimum or a cover from $5-$20. Parking is available at the Hyatt and other nearby pay lots.

Hours: Sunday-Monday 7 p.m., Tuesday-Friday 9 p.m., Saturday 8 p.m., 9 p.m., 10 p.m.

The Groundlings

7307 Melrose Ave., Los Angeles

(323) 934-4747

http://www.groundlings.com

This legendary comedy troupe launched the careers of Lisa Kudrow, Phil Hartman, Chris

The Groundlings (Continued....)

Kattan, Will Farrell, Cheri O'Teri. You're guaranteed to laugh at the next up-and-coming bunch of superstar comedians. There is valet and some street parking available.

Hours: Wednesday-Saturday 8 p.m. show, Friday-Saturday 10 p.m. show, Sunday 7:30 p.m. show

The Laugh Factory

8001 W. Sunset Blvd., West Hollywood

(323) 656-1336

http://www.laughfactory.com

Since 1979, some of the biggest names in comedy performed here at The Laugh Factory. Some notable performers include Jerry Seinfeld, Rodney Dangerfield, and the Wayans brothers. Tickets run from $12-$15, and valet parking ranges from $5.25-$6.25.

Hours: Monday 8 p.m. show, Tuesday 7:30 p.m. and 9:30 p.m. shows, Wednesday-Thursday 8 p.m , Friday-Saturday 8 p.m., 10 p.m., and 12 a.m., Sunday 8 p.m. and 10 p.m.

What to Do if You're Not 21:

Level 3

Hollywood and Highland Complex

(323) 461-2017

Although Level 3 shed its tamer, under-twenty-one image, students can still check out KIIS FM's Club DV8 on Saturdays. Parking is available in the underground garage. The cover is $10-$20.

Wednesday: Live acts

Friday: DJs

Saturday: Over-18 dance party sponsored by KIIS FM.

Hours: Monday, Wednesday, Friday, Saturday 10 p.m.-2 a.m.

The Echo

1822 Sunset Blvd., Echo Park

(213) 413-8200

http://www.attheecho.com

This all-ages club features theme nights like "Hang the DJ," featuring Britpop and 6U's music. For smokers, to avoid paying the cover charge again every time you step out to smoke, try the new smokers patio. Parking is available on the street.

Hours: Vary

The Roxy Theatre
9009 W. Sunset Blvd., West Hollywood
(310) 276-2222
http://www.theroxyonsunset.com
All ages are welcome in this famous club. Recently renovated, the club is changing the format from local bands to national headliners. The cost varies per show, and the valet costs $7. There is also a paid parking lot across the street.
Hours: 8 p.m.-2 a.m.

Student Favorites:
The Space
Sugar
Circle Bar

Useful Resources for Nightlife:
http://www.goldstarevents.com
http://www.la.com

Bars Close At:
2 a.m.

Primary Areas with Nightlife:
Sunset Boulevard
Hollywood
Santa Monica

Cheapest Place to Get a Drink:
Alibi Room
QC2020

Favorite Drinking Games:
Beer Pong
Card Games (A$$hole)
Century Club
Quarters
Power Hour

Organization Parties
One of the most popular ways to party is to hop on a chartered bus with a bunch of other LMU students. These bus parties take students to L.A. clubs for a night of dancing. Most students show up drunk and come home drunker. Associated Students of LMU also features events like Madness @ Midnight to get students involved in some on-campus socializing. Also, events like the Sunset Concert bring great bands to campus.

Students Speak Out On...
Nightlife

"There are bus parties which I heard are fun and safe. Some Thursday nights a tour bus picks people up and goes to bars and clubs and brings them back home."

Q "Clubs? Well, I'm kind of young for those. It really depends how far you are going. **Parties are mostly sororities and frats.** But there are also bus parties where you go on a bus to a surprise location and party."

Q "**Parties on campus are fun,** especially if they're with your organization or club - definitely things to get involved in!"

Q "L.A. has some great clubs. There's a club on Third Street in Santa Monica that I go to sometimes. **You have to be twenty-one for the good stuff.**"

Q "Parties that are on campus are okay, as long as you hold a party that has free food as an incentive to come. In the beginning of the year, there were these bus parties where there would be a bus that would take people to somewhere in Hollywood. From I what have I heard, it is pretty good, and **people end up drunk usually before the bus leaves the campus.** I don't know much about great clubs, but my best bet would be the entire Sunset Strip."

Q "Some of the twenty-one and over clubs are **more chill than the eighteen and over.**"

Q "The bus parties are crazy. So much fun, but if you want to avoid regretting it in the morning, **don't schedule early classes on Friday.** They are worth it if your grade doesn't depend on the success of your hangover remedy. The bus parties are boring unless you are tipsy, to say the least, but most people drink beforehand to avoid the four dollar shots at the bar. I tended to think that the most scantily clad outfit I could come up with still looked like I wore too much material. In other words, the girls are a little scandalous, and the boys like it that way, so be prepared for the shock of PDA (public displays of affection)."

Q "ASLMU throws some good parties, but the best time can be found off campus. I went to a few of the bus parties and then missed my Friday morning class. Not good! But **it was a fun time."**

The College Prowler Take On...
Nightlife

If you are over twenty-one, the city offers an incredible list of hot spots frequented by Hollywood's A-list. While you may not get into the VIP room without a famous friend, there is still a good time to be had at the many unique places in the city. Sunset Strip and Hollywood Boulevard feature a ton of clubs, from dancing to DJs. Closer to home, try Santa Monica and West Los Angeles. Although you may not run into the rich and famous in Santa Monica, you can party with surfers and other college kids just coming off the beach. Bring a friend; some areas of Hollywood and Sunset are pretty seedy.

Some LMU students who are under twenty-one obtain a fake I.D., while others check out the under-twenty-one nights at some popular L.A. spots. The Roxy is open to all ages, so drop in to this legendary club, and you may see the Osbournes. Other spots like Level 3 throw special parties for adults under twenty-one. Los Angeles offers plenty of other options like cozy beachfront cafes and first-rate comedy clubs. Regardless of age, there are plenty of restaurants open late for the midnight crowd. If you're bored in L.A., you just aren't trying hard enough. Websites, city guides, and the phone book provide excellent listings of unusual events.

The College Prowler™ Grade on

Nightlife: A+

A high grade in Nightlife indicates that there are many bars and clubs in the area that are easily accessible and affordable. Other determining factors include the number of options for the under-21 crowd and the prevalence of house parties.

Greek Life

The Lowdown On...
Greek Life

Number of Fraternities:
5

Number of Sororities:
7

Percent of Undergrad Men in Fraternities:
4%

Percent of Undergrad Women in Sororities:
10%

Fraternities on Campus:
Alpha Delta Gamma
Lambda Chi Alpha
Sigma Chi
Sigma Lambda Beta
Sigma Phi Epsilon

Sororities on Campus:
Alpha Phi
Delta Gamma
Delta Sigma Theta
Delta Zeta
Kappa Alpha Theta
Pi Beta Phi
Sigma Lambda Gamma

Other Greek Organizations:
Greek Council
Greek Peer Advisors
Interfraternity Council
Order of Omega
Panhellenic Council

Did You Know?

Delta Gamma's event "Anchor Splash" raises money for Blind Children's Center of Los Angeles.

In the 2002-2003 school year, LMU's Greek community volunteered for 6,229 hours of service and **raised $57,934 for charity.**

The Western Regional Greek Leadership Association awarded LMU's Greek community with **three awards in 2003**: Excellence in Scholastic Achievement and Programming, Most Interfraternal Relations, and the Legacy Award for "sustained excellence and growth."

The LMU chapter of Alpha Phi became the highest fundraising chapter in the nation when members raised more than **$32,000 in November 2003**. The funds benefited the nonprofit organization Caring for Children and Family with Aids and the Alpha Phi Foundation.

Students Speak Out On...
Greek Life

"The Greek scene is big here, but I think that's because a lot of people who wouldn't normally rush at a place like USC or Pepperdine feel comfortable rushing here. LMU is a little more friendly."

Q "It does not dominate the social scene. **There are some cliques,** but you basically do your own thing. It's chill."

Q "Greeks are prevalent. It's either y**ou're in one, you're in a club, or you're no**t. There is a barrier, but it's not too harmful."

Q "Greek life is huge here. Unlike other universities where the Greeks live in a house and their activities are basically unheard of, the Greeks here are very involved in the school and have many public events. There are no Greek houses, and **Greeks live among non-Greeks on campus.** I would also say that the majority of my friends got into a sorority their freshman year, which has inspired me to rush next year, something I never thought I would do when I was in high school! Many of those same friends also never thought they were the 'sorority type,' and now they absolutely love it."

Q "During sorority and fraternity recruitment, it seems as though the whole campus is in a Greek organization, but that is far from the truth. It does not dominate the social scene like at USC. About **less than half of the student body is in a Greek organization**. For the most part, Greek organizations at LMU do not follow the stereotypical view of Greek life that is portrayed in movies. From what I heard, it is pretty mellow."

Q "Almost every girl you see has a sweatshirt with Greek letters on it, and all the guys are wearing their little pledge pins. So **it is somewhat dominating**, but there are enough people that don't care about it to save you from going insane if you aren't a Greek geek."

Q "They seem to have **a strong connection with many students.**"

Q "The best way to get to know any of the fraternities on campus is to **just go and talk with the members.**"

Q "I'm not into the whole Greek thing, but I don't think they're too dominating. Some of the sororities are really cliquey and snotty, but **the frat guys just seem to blend together.**"

Q "Some of my friends are in frats or sororities, and it's really no big deal here. At some schools, Greeks won't socialize with anyone outside of the Greek community, but **at LMU, they are forced to blend in**. There is no fraternity row or anything, so they have to live with the rest of us."

The College Prowler Take On...
Greek Life

At first glance, Greek sweatshirts seem to be a wardrobe staple at LMU. However, the shirts are the most noticeable sign of a Greek community on campus. Like everything else at LMU, the sororities and frats are low-key. Students do not feel Greek life is a prerequisite to popularity, so there isn't too much pressure to participate. Students who choose to rush usually enjoy the Greek experience. Formals, parties, and competitions are a part of the scene, along with a service element. Most organizations hold a yearly philanthropy event to benefit a charitable organization. LMU chapters, most notably Alpha Phi, typically raise thousands of dollars to benefit various causes. Some Greek organizations focus more on academics and service, while others focus on partying, so students with varying interests can find an organization to fit their personalities.

For students who choose not to rush, campus Christian groups, media outlets, and social clubs are a strong element in the LMU social scene. Although Greeks tend to be loyal to other Greeks and Greek life, students who don't join will not be alone. Service organizations like Belles are just as selective as some sororities, while cultural clubs like De Colores provide the same close-knit ties. LMU has a space for you regardless of your attitude towards Greek life.

B+

The College Prowler™ Grade on
Greek Life: B+

A high grade in Greek Life indicates that sororities and fraternities are not only present, but also active on campus. Other determining factors include the variety of houses available and the respect the Greek community receives from the rest of the campus.

Drug Scene

The Lowdown On...
Drug Scene

Most Prevalent Drugs on Campus:
Alcohol
Marijuana
Caffeine
Ritalin

Liquor-Related Referrals:
163

Liquor-Related Arrests:
0

Drug-Related Referrals:
60

Drug-Related Arrests:
0

Drug Counseling Programs

The Student Handbook details the health risks of drug and alcohol consumption, along with the punishments used by the university.

Resident Advisors conduct alcohol abuse prevention programs for dorm residents.

Orientation leaders act out sketches and give lectures about alcohol and drug abuse for incoming students.

Students can attend an Al-Anon meeting at the Student Health Center.

Campus recreation recently started a Balanced Life campaign to promote healthy lifestyles, including healthy eating, exercise, and abstinence from alcohol and drugs.

Once Public Safety cites a student for alcohol possession, the student must attend the school's Alcohol 101 program about the dangers of drugs and alcohol.

Students Speak Out On...
Drug Scene

"I am very surprised when I hear about drugs on campus. I knew one guy, and I heard he got expelled for possession of marijuana, but that's all I know."

"I've not heard anyone mentioning anything about junkies. It's probably something discrete. Alcohol is another story. All I can say is that it's something that EMTs respond to 90% of the time."

"LMU is not a dry campus, but it's not overtaken by drugs. As far as drugs go, it's all about potheads. If anyone is caught with a drug, it is usually marijuana. A ton of people smoke, but cigarettes are not considered an illegal drug. There are very few cases of those heavy drugs used, but it is usually those potheads."

"Oh, everyone drinks, it seems. But alcohol abuse, especially underage, is a huge problem at all colleges. Too many of my high school friends have formed their new life around parties and drinking and 'funny alcohol stories.' I can't say I haven't sipped at one or two parties, but some people really take it over the limit. Our Charter Ball had like twenty-three emergency calls and like ten people admitted to the emergency room in emergency condition because of alcohol abuse. That's pretty sad. As for other drugs, however, they're far more unheard of."

"I have two friends who smoke marijuana, but only on occasion. Most others have never even tried it."

Q "Everybody here drinks. I'm just amazed more people don't get caught. Drugs, though, are not as big. **Some people smoke pot**, but mostly everybody just spends tons of money on coffee when cramming for exams."

Q "A couple of girls in one of my classes used Ritalin so that they could concentrate. I guess that is becoming a bigger thing around here, but **it's still pretty underground.**"

Q "No matter how hard the university tries to control it, alcohol is a big problem here. Drinking a few beers occasionally is one thing, but **so many people take it too far and end up in the hospital.** Then, they get kicked out of school."

Q "**Most of the campus drinks** and shows up to class hung over. What else would you expect? It's college."

The College Prowler Take On...
Drug Scene

College campuses are typically overflowing with alcohol and drug problems, and LMU is no different. Most students drink, and some students drink heavily. It was no surprise to many students when the annual Charter Ball was canceled after numerous alcohol-related emergencies. Even students over twenty-one need to exercise caution when drinking because students caught drinking around minors will end up being hauled into Judicial Affairs. On the positive side, the university does host some events with alcohol for seniors over twenty-one.

Drugs are not a significant problem when compared to alcohol. It seems like everyone knows someone who smokes pot in the dorms, and public safety usually responds to calls about student drug use every few weeks. However, it is very unlikely that you will find a student who openly admits to smoking marijuana or trying other illegal drugs because of the severe penalties from the university. Students looking to satisfy a drug habit will find that scene on campus, but it may take some digging around. If you want to party hard and drink until you pass it out, then you'll find a party, on or off campus, that keeps the beer flowing. However, students who are not interested in the drug scene can avoid it easily.

The College Prowler™ Grade on

Drug Scene: B+

A high grade in the Drug Scene indicates that drugs are not a noticeable part of campus life; drug use is not visible, and no pressure to use them seems to exist.

Campus Strictness

The Lowdown On...
Campus Strictness

What Are You Most Likely to Get Caught Doing on Campus?

Underage drinking

Cheating

Smoking pot

Parking illegally

Speeding

Illegally downloading copyrighted music

Students Speak Out On...
Campus Strictness

"Well, it's kind of strict, I think. I wouldn't know because I haven't been in trouble. You do get written up which includes a fine and court day, and you get expelled after the third offense or automatically, depending on the situation."

"Public Safety says that they're are extremely strict, but stuff still happens. I know for alcohol abuse and DUI's, you have to take an Alcohol 101 course after you have been in Judicial Affairs. **The punishments vary.** Every time I see the Loyolan's Campus Crime Watch section, the biggest thing is underage drinking, and if it is still happening, then I assume not much has been done or reinforced to eradicate the situation."

"Extremely strict, which is good. If you're caught drinking or doing something stupid, you're documented, and they may even let your parents know about it! Even though it's so common, they don't let any underage drinking 'crime' go ignored. Every single one of them goes through the process of being documented and stuff."

"**They are too strict here**. If you get caught drinking, you have to write a letter to your parents explaining what you did. I don't even want to know what they do for anything worse than that."

"Public Safety watches over everything, so if you're going to drink, be quiet. **They bust loud parties,** and you'll end up in Judicial Affairs."

Q "Yes, it's strict, but not as strict as a school like Pepperdine. There are no rules about guys being in the girls' dorms at night. Even though LMU is a dry campus, **the university does sponsor events for seniors over twenty-one.** They try to be somewhat reasonable."

Q "I always here about one student who got expelled for smoking pot, but I never really hear what happens to students who get caught drinking**. I'm guessing they have a 'three strikes and you're out' policy,** but I'm not sure."

Q "**My biggest problem is parking tickets.** You can get a ticket for anything here, even not parking completely in the lines. Alcohol and drug policies are really strict."

Q "It's very strict. **They don't let you get away with anything.**"

The College Prowler Take On...
Campus Strictness

In spite of LMU's squeaky-clean Catholic school image, the students tend to get wild at times. Drinking, cheating, and speeding are all offenses with a various range of penalties. Speeding or other traffic violations result in a heavy fine, but more serious offenses like alcohol abuse and dishonesty land the offender in Judicial Affairs. Cheating is especially serious at LMU; the school employs a plagiarism investigator, and most professors at least threaten to use it.

At times, the campus seems overly strict. Public Safety officers are not lenient, so getting caught violating any of the university's numerous policies results in varying degrees of trouble. Students who end up in the Judicial Affairs system face fines, suspension, or expulsion. Some serious offenses include underage drinking, drug possession, drug use, cheating, reckless driving, and assault. Of these offenses, underage drinking and drug possession are the most common. Lesser offenses include phone or Internet harassment, minor theft, speeding, parking violations, and the general term "suspicious activity." Incidents involving violent crime are almost nonexistent. Due to the crackdown on alcohol and drug abuse on campus, students should exercise caution and common sense. Public Safety and Judicial Affairs are not known for being lenient.

The College Prowler™ Grade on

Campus
Strictness: C

A high Campus Strictness grade implies an overall lenient atmosphere; police and RAs are fairly tolerant, and the administration's rules are flexible.

Parking

The Lowdown On...
Parking

Student Parking Lot?
Yes

Freshman Allowed to Park?
Yes

Parking Permit Cost:
Free

Vehicles that Require Registration with Public Safety:
Cars
Bicycles
Motorcycles
Scooters
Mopeds

→

Best Places to Find a Parking Spot:

University Hall

Good Luck Getting a Parking Spot Here:

Parking Lot A (visitor lot) after 10 a.m.

Drollinger

Parking Lots G and H.

Common Parking Tickets:

Expired Meter: No meters on campus

No Parking Zone: $50

Handicapped Zone: $200 plus the vehicle will be towed.

Fire Hydrant: $100

Illegal Parking: $50

Carpool Only: $50

Tow-Away Zone: $100 plus the vehicle will be towed.

Bike Lane: $100 plus the vehicle will be towed.

Parking Permits

Parking permits are available for all students, faculty, and staff for free. To obtain a parking permit, go to Public Safety in Daum Hall with your student ID and vehicle registration. Students can park in specific on-campus lots depending on their dorm, and all students can park in University Hall and the visitor lot. However, parking on campus requires time and patience because spaces fill up fast, especially in Parking Lot A and the Drollinger Parking Garage. Your best bet? Park in University Hall's P2 and P3 where there are typically several dozen open spots at any given time.

Students Speak Out On...
Parking

"We park for free. Other schools pay hundreds or even thousands of dollars for a parking permit, but here, it's included in tuition. There aren't enough spaces on the main end of campus, but I'd rather drive around for awhile than pay extra."

"Oh, ugh! Parking behind Rosecrans, Desmond, Whelan, and the Loyola Apartments is bad! There were times when it would take me forty minutes to find a parking space! That was infuriating. I do believe that there needs to be more parking located behind these dorms and residences. Perhaps building a parking structure on the main back lot of parking that is there now, maybe **two or three floors of parking would help a lot!"**

"The parking scene is getting worse year after year. That is only because students are lazy and want to park near their dorms. **University Hall has at least 1,000 spot**s and there is always an open spot at every time during the day. Students that live in dorms have their special parking, which makes it difficult for parking. Many times they are paranoid. They will use every alternative to not use a car, so they can keep their parking spot because once they leave the spot, they will never get it back."

"Students here are bad drivers. **My car was dented twice in one semester,** and nobody bothers to stop. I guess stop signs are optional."

"The availability depends what time of day. **It's first come, first serve."**

Q "**Parking is free!!** I've heard that parking was once abundant on campus, but because of the huge size of the freshman class, now if you don't know the right times to park, you won't get any parking - and the wrong time to park in any residential area is weekday mornings after 9 a.m. One morning of a final exam, I came back from a friend's off-campus apartment (where we had spent the whole night studying,) and I was late for my final because the only spot I could find on the entire East side of campus was a thirty minute visitor parking. I finished the final within twenty minutes, but by the time I got back to my car, there was already a nice ticket. Anyway, University Hall, where most of the classrooms are, has a parking garage that never runs out of parking, so that's fine if you're going to class. But if you want to park close to your dorm, you have to return from your weekend the night before unless you want to miss your morning classes!"

Q "I hate it. The dorm lots are the worst. Drollinger is dark and scary. Be careful there at night because it's hard to see, and some really scary people hang out there. **I hear the commuters always complaining about parking in the visitor lot.** I guess it's always packed."

Q "Parking is fine. **Yeah, it's hard to find a spot, but we do it for free. I** know friends who go to other schools who pay $75 for the cheapest parking pass and that gets them a spot at an off-campus location where they take a shuttle to campus. So the fact that we can park in different areas on campus for free, no matter how hard it is sometimes, is awesome!"

The College Prowler Take On...
Parking

The general attitude among students at LMU is that parking is huge problem that is quickly getting out of control. Public safety assigns students to a specific lot depending on their dorm, while commuter students are stuck in University Hall or the visitor lot. Parking generally requires a little bit of luck and a little bit of patience. It is not uncommon for students to drive around for thirty minutes to an hour in search of a spot; however, the parking garage at University Hall usually has spaces available at all times. The downside to University Hall? As the most recent building acquired by LMU, U-Hall is separate from the rest of the campus and requires about an eight-minute walk to the main buildings on Alumni Mall.

On the positive side, parking at LMU is free, but students cannot register more than one vehicle. However, on the negative side, a parking permit does not guarantee a parking space, so there is usually a shortage of spaces for the number of cars on campus. Additionally, as the university admits larger freshman classes each year, the parking situation worsens, but the university has no plans to address it. Parking tickets at LMU are high, with no fine under $50. Public safety patrols the campus at all times to catch violators of the strict parking statutes. When parking at LMU, remember that the free parking permit does come at the price of added frustration and higher parking tickets.

The College Prowler™ Grade on

Parking: C

A high grade in this section indicates that parking is both available and affordable, and that parking enforcement isn't overly severe.

Transportation

The Lowdown On...
Transportation

Ways to Get Around Town

On Campus

The university does not offer a daily shuttle service for students because it takes a maximum of five minutes to get to any building on campus. Considering that students never have to trudge through snow and ice to get to class, the walk is not torturous. However, students with an injury that makes walking difficult can call Public Safety for a ride.

Public Transportation

Santa Monica's Big Blue Bus, (310) 415-5444. Look for the blue triangle signs.

Taxi Cabs

Bell Cab (800) 272-2355

Beverly Hills Cab Co., (800) 273-6611

Northwest Yellow Cab, (310) 659-0105

Taxi! Taxi! (310) 826-2233

United Independent Taxi, (310) 821-1000

→

Car Rentals

Alamo, local: (310) 319-3434; national: (800) 327-9633,

www.alamo.com

Avis, local: (310) 823-7733; national: (800) 831-2847,

www.avis.com

Budget, local: (310) 821-8200; national: (800) 527-0700,

www.budget.com

Dollar, national: (800) 800-4000. www.dollar.com

Enterprise, local:

(310) 827-7800; national: (800) 736-8222, www.enterprise.com

Hertz, local: (310) 568-3400; national: (800) 654-3131,

www.hertz.com

National, local: (310) 338-8200; national: (800) 227-7368,

www.nationalcar.com

Best Ways to Get Around Town:

Los Angeles is home to a massive freeway system, so bring a car and lots of patience.

A bicycle

Lion Express shuttle

Santa Monica Blue Bus

Ways to Get Out of Town:

Airlines Serving Los Angeles:

Aero California, (800) 237-6225

Aeromexico, (800) 237-6639

Air Canada, (888) 247-2262, www.aircanada.com

Air New Zealand,

(800) 262-1234

Alaska Airlines, (800) 252-7522

America West Airlines,

(800) 235-9292

American Airlines,

(800) 433-7300, www.americanairlines.com

British Airways, (800) 247-9297, www.britishairways.com

Continental, (800) 523-3273, www.continental.com

Delta, (800) 221-1212, www.delta-air.com

JetBlue, (800) 538-2583, www.jetblue.com

Lufthansa, (800) 645-3880, www.lufthansa-usa.com

Southwest, (800) 435-9792, www.southwest.com

US Airways, (800) 428-4322, www.usairways.com

United Airlines, (800) 241-6522

United, (800) 241-6522,

www.united.com

US Airways, (800) 428-4322, www.usairways.com

Virgin Atlantic Airways,

(800) 862-8621

Airport:

Los Angeles International Airport (LAX),

LAX is approximately five miles and ten minutes driving time away from Loyola Marymount.

How to Get There:

Northwest Yellow Cab,

(310) 659-0105. Airport Discount 20%

SkyCar, (310) 822-9955

Super Shuttle, (310) 782-6600

United Independent Taxi, (310) 821-1000

A Cab Ride to the Airport Costs:

$12-$14

Greyhound

The Greyhound Bus Terminal is in downtown Los Angeles at 1716 East 7th Street. For more information, call:

(213) 629-8405.

Travel Agents

AAA Automobile Club of Southern California, 1900 S. Sepulveda Blvd., West Los Angeles, (310) 914-8500

Flight Centre, 1229 Wilshire Blvd., Santa Monica,

(310) 458-3310

Flight Centre, 80 Windward Ave., Venice, (310) 450-6239

Global Network Travel, 8651 Lincoln Blvd., Los Angeles, (310) 410-3990

Marina Travel, 4762 Admirality Way, Marina del Rey,

(310) 821-0761

Pacific Heights Travel, 207 Culver Blvd., Playa del Rey, (310) 306-9717

Students Speak Out On...
Transportation

"There are buses, but I haven't heard good things about it. It's L.A., and you need a car. That's pretty much the bottom line."

Q "Starting this year, LMU started this Lion Express. It is a shuttle that takes a limited amount of students to several places such as the Howard Hughes Promenade, Santa Monica, Manhattan Beach, etc. This beats the ghastly public transportation of the MTA metro. As a Los Angeles native, I know the feeling of waiting for such a long time for the bus to come to the stop. Personally, **I think the drivers do not care at all what time they come.** In other words, public transportation makes you hate Los Angeles even more when you first arrive. The best way to beat it is in one of two ways: The Lion Express or get your own car, because the public transportation is as reliable as a shanty house."

Q "I've heard **the Santa Monica Big Blue Bus is great,** but I've never personally taken it. LMU has its own bus too, the Lion Express, but it doesn't go to too many places."

Q "**We have the Lion Express** which transports you to nearby stores, restaurants, and attractions. There's also the Santa Monica Blue Bus, so it's there."

Q "Yikes! L.A. has a lot of traffic. There is the Lion Express that goes around the neighborhood and works as a taxi. Otherwise, **you could always call a real taxi.**"

Q "Learn the bus system if you don't have a car. **The Santa Monica Blue Bus #3 line starts at LAX and ends at UCLA.** It stops by the Third Street Promenade and other places, too. It's great, and it picks you up right in front of University Hall."

Q "The Lion Express is pretty good if you don't have a car. **They are usually late,** though, and they won't pick you up if you miss the last shuttle."

Q "Find a friend with a car, or bring your own. L.A. is easy to get around if you're from here, but if you don't know the area, **it's kind of scary.** Get a map and learn how to get to the good places in Hollywood, downtown, Santa Monica, and South Bay."

Q "Cabs are expensive unless you're going to LAX. We're lucky to be close to the airport, so it is not too expensive or far away to get out of here. I've never tried the public transportation around here, but **the Blue Bus goes all over Santa Monica and Marina del Rey."**

The College Prowler Take On...
Transportation

Los Angeles offers many ways to get in, around, and out of town. For in-town transportation, your best bet is your own car; however, be warned that the L.A. freeway system is not for the faint of heart. Rush hour begins at 3:30 p.m. and ends well after 6 p.m., so any trip on a freeway involves major traffic congestion, accidents, and the occasional police chase. To navigate the area surrounding LMU, try the Lion Express shuttle, a service offered by the university to transport students to popular sites in Santa Monica, Manhattan Beach, and West Los Angeles. Other options include the Santa Monica Big Blue Bus, like the Jim Morrison song. For out-of-town transportation, you can't do much better than LAX, one of the world's busiest airports. Almost every airline imaginable flies into this airport, so it is usually crowded. To avoid the stress of airport traffic, take a cab.

If you're looking to reach a specific site in L.A., chances are there is a bus to take you there. However, buses frequently run late or at odd hours, so a car is always a plus. For out-of-towners, consider befriending a student from the area. Often, they can provide valuable shortcuts to traveling around the city.

B-

The College Prowler™ Grade on
Transportation: B-

A high grade for Transportation indicates that campus buses, public buses, cabs, and rental cars are readily-available and affordable. Other determining factors include proximity to an airport and the necessity of transportation.

Weather

The Lowdown On...
Weather

Average Temperature		Average Precipitation	
Fall:	74 °F	Fall:	0.58 in.
Winter:	66 °F	Winter:	2.63 in.
Spring:	67 °F	Spring:	1.09 in.
Summer:	75 °F	Summer:	0.08 in.

Students Speak Out On...
Weather

> **"One thing that Southern Cali is known for is its weather. It's always perfect, but it does get chilly and foggy on certain days because we're close to the beach, and we're on a bluff. We get some high winds sometimes, but it depends on the season."**

"Beautiful, sunny California. What more can I say? It is hot in the summer but can be a little cool near the beach. **The winter can get cold but not really cold**, especially if you're from the east. Bring jeans, t-shirts, sweaters, rain gear, party clothes and all your trendiest outfits. That is unless you're from L.A., like me, and are over the 'I want to fit in' stage."

"I would say g**enerally warm with lots of chilly wind.** Most people wear spaghetti strap tank tops and miniskirts with no problem, but I usually bring a light jacket wherever I'm going. During the winter it's colder, but not too bad at all, because it's California!"

"The weather is wonderful. The weather here is just perfect. Sometimes, it can get really cold and hot, but that is only in a few instances. The clothing would not consist of tons of winter clothes and tons of parkas. A few windbreaker jackets for when it rains. Apparently, **flip-flops are year-round.** I have seen people in the rain with flip-flops. A lot of summer and spring clothing with a few winter clothes and you're pretty much set."

"**It gets surprisingly cold up on the bluff,** so bring your winter wear, but in the spring LMU begins to meet the Los Angeles stereotype of sun and fun."

Q "Weather during the spring and early summer months can range from the mid-70's to the 90's, so for these months cool clothing is highly recommended. **During the fall and winter it can get quite cool** into the 40's and 50's. Turtlenecks, jackets, sweaters, and sweats are good to have handy. You can always change if need be."

Q **"I just love the weather here**. I'm from the Midwest, so I'm used to two feet of snow on the ground in January. Now, I wear shorts in the winter."

Q "LMU is on a hill just off the coast, so we do get a strong ocean breeze. It gets pretty cold sometimes, so bring some sweatshirts. **You'll need an umbrella for when it rains."**

Q "It's usually in the mid-70's here, so it's pretty mild. **It's colder in the mornings and on days when it's foggy**, but usually around noon it warms up."

Q "Perfect. Oh, sure, **there are days when it's chilly, but I'm not complaining.** Nobody here really needs heavy coats or air conditioning. The temperature is pretty much the same year round."

The College Prowler Take On...
Weather

One word: Sunshine. Although it is a stereotype, California is the land of sun and surf with little variance in seasons. If you are from the eastern half of the nation, a winter without snow and ice is bizarre. Instead, California winters are much like the other seasons: mild and sunny. In the winter months, precipitation comes in the form of a deluge of rain; often, the city receives a month's allotment of rain in two or three days. While the rest of the nation suffers with arctic cold fronts, Californians deal with some light wind and rain. Although Los Angeles lacks winter weather, fashionable Angelenos break out the winter coats and Ugg boots when the temperature dips below sixty-five degrees.

The coastal areas, including LMU, are breezier than the rest of the city. In the mornings, a blanket of sea fog covers the area, but it usually dissipates in the afternoon. For the cooler, breezier days, a sweatshirt or coat is highly recommended, although some students still wear T-shirts and shorts. L.A. is one of the few cities in the nation where students don't need to worry about walking to class in the snow.

A

The College Prowler™ Grade on

Weather: A

A high Weather grade designates that temperatures are mild and rarely reach extremes, that the campus tends to be sunny rather than rainy, and that weather is fairly consistent rather than unpredictable.

Report Card Summary

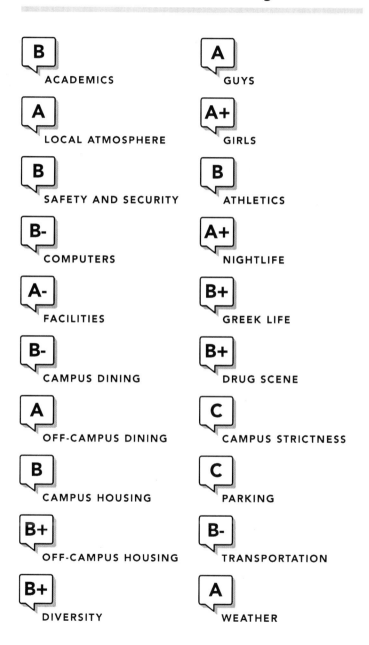

B ACADEMICS

A LOCAL ATMOSPHERE

B SAFETY AND SECURITY

B- COMPUTERS

A- FACILITIES

B- CAMPUS DINING

A OFF-CAMPUS DINING

B CAMPUS HOUSING

B+ OFF-CAMPUS HOUSING

B+ DIVERSITY

A GUYS

A+ GIRLS

B ATHLETICS

A+ NIGHTLIFE

B+ GREEK LIFE

B+ DRUG SCENE

C CAMPUS STRICTNESS

C PARKING

B- TRANSPORTATION

A WEATHER

Overall Experience

Students Speak Out On...
Overall Experience

"I like LMU! I have experienced some difficulties with LMU's administration and learning where and who to contact in particular situations. This can be very frustrating! However, with time, things have improved, and college truly is a new life to live and explore!"

"So far, I really enjoy the size of LMU. I like that I see at least one person I know every time I walk out of my dorm room. **Everyone is really friendly and the environment is beautiful,** clean and comfortable. You feel like you are taken care of here. The teachers are caring, and despite a few bad seeds, LMU is a great place."

Q "Personally, **I am pretty content at LMU.** Almost all my experiences from professors to students to student center have only been good. Students seemed to be laid-back, relaxed, mellow, and friendly which really helps when coming on to campus every day because you do not feel so alienated. LMU is in such a wonderful area, and the atmosphere is pretty lively. My only complaint is the efficiency of the administration, especially in financial aid. **They are very disorganized,** which is not good; that can really turn off prospective students. I am happy to be where I am at because I know I would not have this experience at any other college, which makes me feel good in deciding to come to LMU."

Q "**This was my first choice and it still stands as my first choice**, even though my parents still wish I had gone elsewhere. The best thing about LMU is how small it is. So many things come from a school being small—more attention to the individual, smaller classes. You don't feel swallowed up as a freshman, and there's no complicated parking permits and stuff like that."

Q "Well, at first it was very frightening, not knowing anything. You just somehow find a way to know your way around the system. At the beginning, I wanted to be somewhere else, because **I thought I wouldn't fit in socially or intellectually, but I soon adjusted**. There are times when things are just too new to make the effort of getting used to it, like classes."

Q "Fun! I love LMU! **I could never go anywhere else**. It's expensive but worth it. Even more worth it if you have scholarships, grants and loans!"

Q "I almost transferred because I felt like the school was too small, but now, I'm glad I stayed. My first choice was USC, but I'm happy here. I feel like I **know more people here than I would everywhere else.**"

Q "**We pay a ton of money**—$35,000—to go here, and I think I see where that money goes. The buildings are beautiful, and most of my classes are useful. I like the liberal arts end of it."

Q "This is a tight-knit school. You can't just hide in a crowd because there aren't any. While you get to know everyone, sometimes there is a huge pressure to fit in—have the right clothes, right car. **Sometimes it's intimidating**, but I'm happy with the atmosphere."

Q "To make it here, you have to find your place. Find people with the same interests and beliefs and also branch out and meet new people. I think LMU provides enough clubs and activities and classes to do that. Yeah, **we're not USC or UCLA, but I think that's a good thing.** We have our own identity."

The College Prowler Take On...
Overall Experience

Students here are quick to point out that LMU differs from its neighbors USC and UCLA. Overall, LMU is quiet and intimate. Palm trees dot the courtyards between the small buildings. On the exterior, LMU looks like an expensive school. The grounds are neatly manicured and constantly maintained. The school lacks the concrete sterility of a major university, but it possesses the advantages of a big city school—theaters, museums, celebrities. The biggest contributor to student satisfaction is the size. Students cite a small student body and close ties with professors as the main advantages to an LMU education. Another plus is the lavish facilities, especially the Burns Rec Center with its state-of-the-art fitness center. The academics programs are also a highlight with students. The film school is growing in size and notoriety, while programs in political science, business, and communications are strong points.

On the negative side, a small university still possesses the same problems of a large university. Students repeatedly report problems with a disorganized administration, especially financial aid. Parking and housing are increasing problems that the university is only beginning to address through the addition of new residence halls. LMU is not perfect, but no university is. For students searching for a small, private university, LMU offers advantages that few other universities can provide, namely, a friendly, socially conscious student body and a curriculum to match.

The Inside Scoop

The Lowdown On...
The Inside Scoop

LMU Slang

Know the slang, know the school. The following is a list of things you really need to know before coming to LMU. The more of these words you know, the better off you'll be.

The Book: Every entering freshman class must read a particular book selected by the university and attend a lecture by the author. Professors then use that book for essay writing in the required college writing course.

The Coffee Cart: A small snack stand between Foley and Seaver that provides students with a between-class caffeine fix.

Convo: Tuesday and Thursday from 12 p.m. to 1:30 p.m. No classes are scheduled for this time, so students have a chance to catch some great bands and speakers, and most importantly, free food!

First-Year: This is the LMU term for freshman. Second, third, and fourth year students are still called sophomores, juniors, and seniors.

The Fu: (pronounced Foo) The Furama Hotel on Lincoln Blvd.

The Lair: The main dining hall at LMU.

Lion Mail: Student e-mail accounts. This differs from the mail system that the faculty and staff use.

One Card: This is your student I.D. and required for almost anything on campus. You need this to buy food, enter the library, work out at the gym. Bad news: your student I.D. number is your social security number. Good news: the school is slowly changing this system to eliminate the use of social security numbers.

The Pond: The fountain outside of Foley. It is an LMU tradition to throw a friend in the Pond on their birthday.

PROWL: PROWL is the online system that allows students to register for classes, apply for financial aid, and view transcripts and final grades.

ROAR: The phone system for course registration

U-Hall: University Hall. The university acquired this building in 2000, and it now houses most of the Bellarmine College of Liberal Arts, Roski Dining Hall, and some classrooms. Many students say going to class in U-Hall is like going to class in a mall.

Things I Wish I Knew Before Coming to LMU

• Check out your professors before signing up for classes. Students with a Lion e-mail account can register on dogears. net to obtain professor ratings. Students also post ratings on www.ratemyprofessors.com.

• Get on the smallest meal plan because in spite of the high price of food, you will have money left over.

• If you use Flexi-dollars, be aware that they charge sales tax, and the tax adds up.

• Bring a refrigerator.

• Don't get rid of your winter clothes before coming to Los Angeles. You may need them.

• Buy tons of bottled water.

• The Lair food looks great the first week and tastes even better. After the first week, it gets old.

Things I Wish I Knew (Continued....)

- Don't let your parents bring a video camera to orientation or else they will film all of the embarrassing ice-breaker games. It will provide years of laughter at your expense.

- Buy books online at Amazon or other online sites.

- Don't expect to get more than a few dollars when selling books back to the bookstore.

- The school is expensive. In addition to tuition and room and board, the cost of books, food, and transportation adds up.

Tips to Succeed at LMU

- Meet as many people as possible in the first few weeks. Even if they don't become close friends, you can guarantee that you will know a few faces in every class.

- Form study groups. You're all in this together, and it is nice to have a friend to complain to.

- Spread the word about good and bad professors.

- Take classes that sound interesting.

- If you're interested, double major. LMU makes it easy to double major, and many students find that the extra work is worth it.

- If you stay out late, do not sign up for an 8 a.m. class.

- Remember that at LMU, you are not just a number. Your professors will know you well, so cheating or showing up late every day does affect your grade.

- Go to office hours or e-mail your professor.

- Join a service organization. You'll meet tons of friendly people and help the community at the same time.

LMU Urban Legends

- A network of tunnels runs underneath Sunken Garden and connects some of the buildings on campus.

- The biggest wine cellar in Southern California is underneath Sunken Garden.

- All of the Jesuit priests, including the university's president, belong to an ancient secret society that meets in the tunnels under Sunken Garden. Some versions of this myth include Mel Gibson in the secret society.

- Some of LMU's employees are convicted felons on a work-release program.

- The ghost of a Jesuit priest haunts Sunken Gardens and mows the lawn.

School Spirit

LMU athletics are not overwhelmingly popular, so school spirit is lacking when it comes to sports. However, school spirit becomes apparent whenever the volleyball team defeats Pepperdine (a major rival.) If you wear an LMU sweatshirt in Los Angeles, a fellow student usually will strike up a conversation with the question, "Don't you just love LMU?" Most students feel a sense of bitterness towards USC, which further united them in a love for LMU.

Traditions

Bellarmine Forum

The Bellarmine Forum is a week long lecture series in late October and early November. Sponsored by the Bellarmine College of Liberal Arts, the university-wide event focuses on a specific topic. Past topics include globalization and ethics, violence, God, and race.

Charter Ball

Each year, LMU hosts a prom-like event to celebrate the merger of Loyola University and Marymount College in 1973. Charter Ball began in 1993, and it became a night marked by alcohol poisoning and drinking binges. In 2004, ASLMU and Student Life attempted to prevent these emergencies by changing Charter Ball's image and implementing strict security measures. However, Charter Ball finally was cancelled after the 2004 event yielded more student trips to the emergency room than previous years. Even though Charter Ball is gone, the 1973 merger will be celebrated with some event.

Hunger Banquet

Get a taste of life in a third-world country. A few participants receive a steak dinner, more receive a box lunch, and the majority eats a meal of rice and beans. The event raises awareness for the lack of food available to the masses in the world's poorer nations.

Justice Tour

Part of the Sunset Concert, the Justice Tour is a symposium that brings students together to discuss pressing political issues that affect the world. The event's first year focused on "The Human Face of Globalization."

Madness @ Midnight

This event marks the beginning of basketball season. It features food, games, and music, plus a chance to cheer for the basketball team.

Sunset Concert

Annual concert to bring bands to play at LMU. The 2003 concert featured Tom Morello (Rage Against the Machine, Audioslave,) Jurassic 5, and the student band Wet Brain.

The Casassa Lecture

Named after former LMU President Charles Casassa, this lecture brings in an influential speaker to inform the university community about pertinent political and religious topics.

Finding a Job or Internship

The Lowdown On...
Finding a Job or Internship

If you have work-study, it is very easy to find a job on campus that fits your interests, schedule, and needs. However, if you are looking for something off campus, then LMU still has services to help you in the search. Career Development Services and Student Employment Services connect students with on and off-campus opportunities. Career Development Services also offers career counseling, interview guide, résumé help, workshops and other events to help you succeed. They will also connect you with online sites like MonsterTrak through Monster.com.

Advice

When looking for a job, it doesn't hurt to be aggressive. For an on-campus position, stop in and inquire about available positions. It shows that you are enthusiastic about working in that department. Also, ask your friends. Students often

Advice (Continued....)

hear about available positions before Student Employment Services. For off-campus jobs, check online or with Career Development Services.

Career Center Resources & Services:

Average Salary Information

The following statistics represent average starting salaries for LMU graduates by major.

- Online searches
- Full-time and part-time job binders
- Career counseling
- Hot Jobs Flyer
- Career Fairs
- Resume Assistance

- Internship Workshops
- Career Exploration Program
- Internship Classes
- CDS Career Library
- Mock Interviews

Bellarmine College of Liberal Arts:

- English (Education): $49,000
- English (Writing): $50,000
- Liberal Studies: $49,000
- Psychology: $30,900
- Theological Studies: $58,000

College of Communication and Fine Arts:

- Art/Multimedia: $39,100
- Dance: $37,000
- Music: $34,000
- Theatre Arts:$53,000

Frank R. Seaver College of Science and Engineering:

- Biology: $42,500
- Electrical Engineering: $55,000
- Natural Science: $35,000

Loyola Law School

$105,000

School of Education

Varies

School of Film and Television:

- Animation: $39,000
- Film Production: $34,900
- Television Production: $34,900
- Recording Arts: $45,000
- Screenwriting: Varies

Firms That Most Frequently Hire Graduates:

Northrup Grumman
- KPMG LLP
- Ernest & Young
- Boeing
- Dreamworks,
- Warner Bros

- Los Angeles Unified School System, Nissan North America
- Price Waterhouse Coopers
- City of Los Angeles environmental engineering Dept

Did You Know?
82% of Loyola Marymount graduates enter the job market within six months of graduation.

Alumni

The Lowdown On...
Alumni

Office:
Alumni Relations
University Hall, Suite 2000
One LMU Drive
Los Angeles, CA 90045-2659
1-866-LMU-ALUM

Website:
http://www.lmu.edu/alumni

Services Available

The Department of Alumni Relations is on the second floor of University Hall in Suite 2000. It is open from 8 a.m. to 5 p.m. and serves a community of 53,000 LMU graduates. Alumni Relations staff plan reunions, benefits, and service opportunities for alumni. They also connect students with alumni mentors.

Major Alumni Events

For one weekend in June, LMU alumni go back to bluffs for the Annual Grand Reunion Weekend. Activities include a service project, reception, microbrew tasting, live entertainment, and a champagne brunch. Alumni Relations also plans the Alumni for Others event, a day of service and reflection that allows LMU grads to connect with the city. Other events include a Lenten Retreat, barbeques, and regional events nationwide.

Alumni Publications

There is an alumni e-newsletter that informs subscribers about upcoming events, extension courses, and important dates.

Did You Know?

Famous LMU Alumni

Tony Bui, producer of the movies "Green Dragon," "Three Seasons," and "Yellow Lotus"

Kim Costello, writer for television shows like "Threat Matrix," "The Division," "The Pretender," and "JAG"

Steve Franks, writer of the film "Big Daddy"

Brian Helgeland, writer/director/producer, Academy Award nominated writer for "Mystic River," and Academy Award winner for "L.A. Confidential." Other credits include "Man on Fire," "The Order," "A Knight's Tale," "Payback," and "Conspiracy Theory."

Tom Huang, director of "Freshman"

Steve McEveety, producer of "The Passion of the Christ"

David Mirkin, director of the movie "Heartbreakers" and "Romy and Michele's High School Reunion" and episodes of "The Larry Sanders Show" and "The Simpsons"

Darin Morgan, writer for "The X-Files" and "Millennium"

Glen Morgan, writer of the film "Final Destination" and the upcoming "Final Destination 3." Also wrote for the television series "The X-Files."

Van Partible, creator of the television series "Johnny Bravo."

James Wong, writer for the upcoming film "Final Destination 3" and the television series "Space: Above and Beyond" and "The X-Files"

Linda Cardelini (Class of '97), star of the television series "Freaks and Geeks"

Kelli Lynn Harrison (Class of '96), writer

Scott Klier (Class of '93), stage manager for the Broadway production of "Sunset Boulevard"

Student Organizations

Accounting Society	http://aslmu.lmu.edu/acctsoc
Alpha Delta Gamma	http://aslmu.lmu.edu/adg
Alpha Phi	http://aslmu.lmu.edu/alphaphi
Alpha Psi Omega	http://aslmu.lmu.edu/apsio-mega
American Society of Civil Engineers	http://aslmu.lmu.edu/asce
American Society of Mechanical Engineers	http://aslmu.lmu.edu/asme
Animation Club: Society of the All Encompassing Art	http://aslmu.lmu.edu/anima-tion
Armenian Student Organization	http://aslmu.lmu.edu/asa
Asian and Pacific Islander Association	http://aslmu.lmu.edu/apsa
Associated Students of LMU	http://aslmu.lmu.edu
Association for Computing Machinery at LMU	http://aslmu.lmu.edu/comp-machine
Auto Enthusiasts	http://aslmu.lmu.edu/autoen-thusiasts
Belles	http://aslmu.lmu.edu/belles

Best Buddies	Promoting friendships for developmentally disabled people
Beta Gamma Sigma	http://aslmu.lmu.edu/beta-gammasigma
Black Student Union	http://aslmu.lmu.edu/bsu
Biotechnology Society	http://aslmu.lmu.edu/biotech-society
Black Pre-Health Organization of LMU	http://aslmu.lmu.edu/blkpre-health
Boardriders Club	http://aslmu.lmu.edu/board-riders
Brothers of Consciousness	http://aslmu.lmu.edu/boc
Business Law Society	http://aslmu.lmu.edu/lawsociety
Campus Christian Fellowship	http://aslmu.lmu.edu/ccf
Chemistry Society	http://aslmu.lmu.edu/chemsoc
Chicanos for Creative Medicine	http://aslmu.lmu.edu/ccm
Club Fusion	http://aslmu.lmu.edu/clubfusion
College Republicans	http://aslmu.lmu.edu/crs
Consort and Concert Choir	http://aslmu.lmu.edu/choir
Creative Student Activists' Collective	http://aslmu.lmu.edu/creative
Crimson Circle	http://aslmu.lmu.edu/crimsoncir
Cycling Club	http://aslmu.lmu.edu/cycling
De Colores	http://aslmu.lmu.edu/decolores
Del Rey Players- http://aslmu.lmu.edu/delreyplayers	
Delta Gamma	http://aslmu.lmu.edu/delta-gamma
Delta Sigma Pi	http://aslmu.lmu.edu/delsigpi
Delta Sigma Theta	http://aslmu.lmu.edu/deltasigtheta
Delta Zeta	http://aslmu.lmu.edu/deltazeta
Economics Society	http://aslmu.lmu.edu/econsoc
El Espejo	http://aslmu.lmu.edu/elespejo

Emergency Medical Services of LMU	http://aslmu.lmu.edu/ems
Feed the Hungry	http://aslmu.lmu.edu/feed-hungry
Filmmakers Society	http://aslmu.lmu.edu/filmmakers
Finance Society	http://aslmu.lmu.edu/finance
Flying Lions	http://aslmu.lmu.edu/flyinglions
Friends of Jesus	http://aslmu.lmu.edu/anawin
Future Teachers Association	http://aslmu.lmu.edu/future-teachers
Gay Straight Alliance	http://aslmu.lmu.edu/gsa
Greek Council	http://aslmu.lmu.edu/greek
Gryphon Circle	http://aslmu.lmu.edu/gryphoncir
Habitat for Humanity	http://aslmu.lmu.edu/habitat4humanity
Han Tao	seeks to promote Chinese culture
Health Advocates	http://aslmu.lmu.edu/healthadv
H.O.P.E.	http://aslmu.lmu.edu/hope
Human Rights Coalition	http://aslmu.lmu.edu/hrc
Ignatians	http://aslmu.lmu.edu/ignatians
Institute of Electric and Electronics Engineers	http://aslmu.lmu.edu/ieee
Isang Bansa	http://aslmu.lmu.edu/isang-bansa
Kappa Alpha Theta	http://aslmu.lmu.edu/kat
KXLU	LMU's radio station
Kyodai	Promotes Japanese-American culture on campus
Lambda Chi Alpha	http://aslmu.lmu.edu/lambdachi
Latino Business Student Association - http://aslmu.lmu.edu/lbsa	
Leftout	http://aslmu.lmu.edu/leftout

LMU TV	http://aslmu.lmu.edu/lmutv
Los Angeles Loyolan	http://loyolan.lmu.edu
Loyola Rugby	http://aslmu.lmu.edu/rugby
Math Club	http://aslmu.lmu.edu/math
Marians	LMU's newest service organization for women
MeChA	http://aslmu.lmu.edu/mecha
Men's Club Soccer	http://aslmu.lmu.edu/soccer
Men's Lacrosse	http://aslmu.lmu.edu/mlacrosse
Middle Eastern Club	Promoting Middle Eastern culture and unity
Mock Trial Team and Pre-Law Society	http://aslmu.lmu.edu/prelaw
Multicultural Club	
Na Kolea	http://aslmu.lmu.edu/nakolea
National Society of Black Engineers	http://aslmu.lmu.edu/nsbe
Natural Science Society	http://aslmu.lmu.edu/naturalscience
Omulu Sul Capoeira Club	Established to develop awareness of the Capoeira
Order of Omega	http://aslmu.lmu.edu/orderomega
Phi Alpha Theta	http://aslmu.edu/phiatheta
Player's Club	http://aslmu.lmu.edu/players
Pi Beta Phi	http://aslmu.lmu.edu/pibetaphi
Political Science Association	http://aslmu.lmu.edu/psa
Pro-Life Association	http://aslmu.lmu.edu/prolife
Psi Chi	http://aslmu.lmu.edu/psichi
Resident Housing Association	
Righteousness in Christ Fellowship	http://aslmu.lmu.edu/rightinchrist
Rotaract Club	http://aslmu.lmu.edu/rotaract
Sankofa Society	http://aslmu.lmu.edu/sankofa
Scuba Club	http://aslmu.lmu.edu/scuba

Service Organization Council	
Sierra Club	http://aslmu.lmu.edu/sierra
Sigma Chi	http://aslmu.lmu.edu/sigmachi
Sigma Lambda Beta	http://aslmu.lmu.edu/lmubetas
Sigma Lambda Gamma	http://aslmu.lmu.edu/sigmalambdagamma
Sigma Phi Epsilon	http://aslmu.lmu.edu/sigep
Sigma Tau Delta	http://aslmu.lmu.edu/sigmataudelta
Sistah Friends	http://aslmu.lmu.edu/sistahfriends
Society of Automotive Engineers	http://aslmu.lmu.edu/socautoeng
Society of Hispanic Professional Engineers	http://aslmu.lmu.edu/shpe
Society of Women Engineers	http://aslmu.lmu.edu/sowe
Sociology Society	http://aslmu.lmu.edu/socsociety
Soul Food: The Ministry	http://aslmu.lmu.edu/soulfood
Spanish Club	http://aslmu.lmu.edu/spanish
Speakeasy	http://aslmu.lmu.edu/speakeasy
Special Games	coordinates and sponsors Special Games at LMU
Student Alumni Association	
Student Athlete Advisory Committee	
Sursum Corda	http://aslmu.lmu.edu/sursumcorda
Swing and Ballroom Club of LMU	http://aslmu.lmu.edu/ballroom
The Defender	http://aslmu.lmu.edu/defender
The Tower Yearbook	
TLC Club	http://aslmu.lmu.edu/tlc
Travel and Tourism Club	
Tri Beta Biological Honors Society	http://aslmu.lmu.edu/tribeta
Volunteer Admissions Team	http://aslmu.lmu.edu/vat

Women for Justice	Educating about issues of female life on and off campus
Women's Lacrosse	http://aslmu.lmu.edu/wla-crosse
Women's Volleyball	http://aslmu.lmu.edu/wvol-leyball
W.O.R.D.U.P.	Women of Racial Diversity Unifying Perspective
Writer's Guild of LMU	http://aslmu.lmu.edu/writers
Young Democrats	http://aslmu.lmu.edu/young-democrats

The Best & The Worst

The Ten BEST Things About LMU:

1 The weather

2 Friendly students

3 Los Angeles

4 Cleanliness—The school hires people to blow the dirt off the sidewalks with leaf blowers.

5 Burns Recreation Center

6 Service organizations that actually do make a difference

7 On-campus film screenings and theater productions

8 University Hall

9 Interesting classes

10 Intelligent, friendly professors

The Ten **WORST** Things About LMU:

1 Disorganized Financial Aid Office

2 Inadequate financial aid

3 Tuition and housing hikes

4 Parking shortage

5 Overcrowding in dorms

6 The Book

7 Hit-and-run accidents in the parking lots

8 Campus food

9 Students who pull the fire alarm at 2 a.m.

10 The Furama Hotel and Westchester

Visiting LMU

The Lowdown On...
Visiting LMU

Hotel Information

LAX:

Comfort Inn and Suites
4922 W. Century Blvd.
Los Angeles, CA 90304
(800) 667-5696
Distance from Campus: 5 miles
Price Range: $65-$85

Courtyard by Marriott
6161 W. Century Blvd.
Los Angeles, CA 90045
(310) 649-1400
Distance from Campus: 5 miles
Price Range: $160-$190

Days Inn
901 W. Manchester Blvd.
Los Angeles, CA 90301
(310) 649-0800
Distance from Campus:
Less than 5 miles
Price Range: $55-$75

Embassy Suites Hotel
9801 Airport Blvd.
Los Angeles, CA 90045
(310) 215-1000
Distance from Campus:
Less than 5 miles
Price Range: $190-$290

Four Points by Sheraton
http://www.fourpointslax.com
9750 Airport Blvd.
Los Angeles, CA 90045
(310) 645-4600
Distance from Campus:
Less than 5 miles
Price Range: $89-$115

Holiday Inn LAX
9901 La Cienega Blvd.
Los Angeles, CA 90045
(310) 649-5151
Distance from Campus: 5 miles
Price Range: $120-$150

Los Angeles Airport Hilton & Towers
5711 W. Century Blvd.
Los Angeles, CA 90045
(310) 410-4000
Distance from Campus: 5 miles
Price Range: $90-$200

Los Angeles Airport Marriott
5855 W. Century Blvd.
Los Angeles, CA 90045
(310) 641-5700
Distance from Campus: 5 miles
Price Range: $120-$200

Super 8 Motel at LAX
9250 Airport Blvd.
Los Angeles, CA 90045
(310) 670-2900
Distance from Campus:
Less than 5 miles
Price Range: $65-$95

Travelodge Hotel at LAX
5547 W. Century Blvd.
Los Angeles, CA 90045
(310) 649-4000
Distance from Campus: 5 miles
Price Range: $65-$110

Marina del Rey:

Best Western-Jamaica Bay Inn
4175 Admiralty Way
Marina del Rey, CA 90292
(310) 823-5333
Distance from Campus:
Less than 5 miles
Price Range: $130-$190

Courtyard by Marriott
13480 Maxella Ave.
Marina del Rey, CA 90292
(310) 822-8555
Distance from Campus:
Less than 5 miles
Price Range: $160

Foghorn Harbor Inn
4140 Via Marina
Marina del Rey, CA 90292
(310) 823-4626
Distance from Campus: 5 miles
Price Range: $110-$160

Marina Beach Marriott Hotel
4100 Admiralty Way
Marina del Rey, CA 90292
(310) 301-3000
Distance from Campus: Less
than 5 miles
Price Range: $170-$230

Marina International Hotel
4200 Admiralty Way
Marina del Rey, CA 90292
(310) 301-2000
Distance from Campus: Less
than 5 miles
Price Range: $100-$120

The Ritz-Carlton, Marina del Rey
4375 Admiralty Way
Marina del Rey, CA 90292
(310) 823-1700
Distance from Campus: 5 miles
Price Range: $240-$600

Westchester:

Furama Hotel
8601 Lincoln Blvd.
Los Angeles, CA 90045
(800) 225-8126
Distance from Campus: Less
than 1 mile
Price Range: $90-$140

Take a Campus Virtual Tour

To Schedule a Group Information Session or Interview

The Admissions Office schedules a limited number of group visits during the year, so make arrangements by September 12 for fall or January 10 for spring. Group visits take place on Monday through Friday between 9 a.m. and 3 p.m., and the groups must consist of fifty students or less. High school students only. Call (310) 338-2750 or (800) 568-4636 for more information.

Campus Tours

Students lead campus tours on Monday through Friday from 10 a.m. to 1 p.m. Tours also begin at 11 a.m. on Saturdays. Hours and availability change during holidays or exam periods. The tours are approximately ninety minutes long and include a session with an admissions advisor.

Overnight Visits

Overnight accommodations are not available for visiting students. However, students accepted to the university can attend a day visit. This program matches freshmen applicants with a current student. Applicants attend classes, take a tour, meet a counselor, visit with faculty, and try the food. The visits are available in February, March, and early April. Space is limited, so interested students must notify the university two weeks in advance. To schedule, call (310) 338-7396 or e-mail LMUDayVisit@yahoo.com.

Directions to Campus

Driving from the North
- Take Lincoln Blvd. south.
- Pass Jefferson Blvd.
- Turn left onto LMU Drive.

Driving from the South
- Take N. Sepulveda Blvd. (HWY 1) north and continue onto Lincoln Blvd.
- Continue for 3.5 miles on Lincoln Blvd.
- Turn right onto LMU Drive.

Driving from the East
- Take I-10 west to I-405 South.
- Take Jefferson Blvd to Lincoln Blvd.
- Turn south on Lincoln Blvd.
- Turn left onto LMU Drive.

Driving from the West
- Take Manchester Blvd. to Lincoln Blvd.
- Turn north on Lincoln Blvd.
- Drive approximately .5 miles.
- Turn right onto LMU Drive.

Words to Know

Academic Probation – A student can receive this if they fail to keep up with their school's academic minimums. Those who are unable to improve their grades after receiving this warning can possibly face dismissal.

Beer Pong / Beirut – A drinking game with numerous cups of beer arranged in a particular pattern on each side of a table. The goal is to get a ping pong ball into one of the opponent's cups by throwing the ball or hitting it with a paddle. If the ball lands in a cup, the opponent is required to drink the beer.

Bid – An invitation from a fraternity or sorority to pledge their specific house.

Blue-Light Phone – Brightly-colored phone posts with a blue light bulb on top. These phones exist for security purposes and are located at various outside locations around most campuses. If a student has an emergency or is feeling endangered, they can pick up one of these phones (free of charge) to connect with campus police or an escort service.

Campus Police – Policemen who are specifically assigned to a given institution. Campus police are not regular city officers; they are employed by the university in a full-time capacity.

Club Sports – A level of sports that falls somewhere between varsity and intramural. If a student is unable to commit to a varsity team but has a lot of passion for athletics, a club sport could be a better, less intense option. If a club sport still requires too much commitment, intramurals often involve no traveling and a lot less time.

Cocaine – An illegal drug. Also known as "coke" or "blow," cocaine often resembles a white crystalline or powdery substance. It is highly addictive and dangerous.

Common Application – An application that students can use to apply to multiple schools.

Course Registration – The time when a student selects what courses they would like for the upcoming quarter or semester. Prior to registration, it is best to have an idea of several back-up courses in case a particular class becomes full. If a course is full, a student can place themselves on the waitlist, although this still does not guarantee entry.

Division Athletics – Athletics range from Division I to Division III. Division IA is the most competitive, while Division III is considered to be the least competitive.

Dorm – Short for dormitory, a dorm is an on-campus housing facility. Dorms can provide a range of options from suite-style rooms to more communal options that include shared bathrooms. Most first-year students live in dorms. Some upperclassmen who wish to stay on campus also choose this option.

Early Action – A way to apply to a school and get an early acceptance response without a binding commitment. This is a system that is becoming less and less available.

Early Decision – An option that students should use only if they are positive that a place is their dream school. If a student applies to a school using the early decision option and is admitted, they are required and bound to attend that university. Admission rates are usually higher with early decision students because the school knows that a student is making them their first choice.

Ecstasy – An illegal drug. Also known as "E" or "X," ecstasy looks like a pill and most resembles an aspirin. Considered a party drug, ecstasy is very dangerous and can be deadly.

Ethernet – An extremely fast internet connection that is usually available in most university-owned residence halls. To use an Ethernet connection properly, a student will need a network card and cable for their computer.

Fake ID – A counterfeit identification card that contains false information. Most commonly, students get fake IDs and change their birthdates so that they appear to be older than 21 (of legal drinking age). Even though it is illegal, many college students have fake IDs in hopes of purchasing alcohol or getting into bars.

Frosh – Slang for "freshmen."

Hazing – Initiation rituals that must be completed for membership into some fraternities or sororities. Numerous universities have outlawed hazing due to its degrading or dangerous requirements.

Sports (IMs) – A popular, and usually free, student activity where students create teams and compete against other groups for fun. These sports vary in competitiveness and can include a range of activities—everything from billiards to water polo. IM sports are a great way to meet people with similar interests.

Keg – Officially called a half barrel, a keg contains roughly 200 12-ounce servings of beer and is often found at college parties.

LSD – An illegal drug. Also known as acid, this hallucinogenic drug most commonly resembles a tab of paper.

Marijuana – An illegal drug. Also known as weed or pot; besides alcohol, marijuana is one of the most commonly found drugs on campuses across the country.

Major –The focal point of a student's college studies; a specific topic that is studied for a degree. Examples of majors include physics, English, history, computer science, economics, business, and music. Many students decide on a specific major before arriving on campus, while others are simply "undecided" and figure it out later. Those who are extremely interested in two areas can also choose to double major.

Meal Block – The equivalent of one meal. Students on a "meal plan" usually receive a fixed number of meals per week.

Each meal, or "block," can be redeemed at the school's dining facilities in place of cash. More often than not, if a student fails to use their weekly allotment of meal blocks, they will be forfeited.

Minor – An additional focal point in a student's education. Often serving as a compliment or addition to a student's main area of focus, a minor has fewer requirements and prerequisites to fulfill than a major. Minors are not required for graduation from most schools; however some students who want to further explore many different interests choose to have both a major and a minor.

Mushrooms – An illegal drug. Also known as "shrooms," this drug looks like regular mushrooms but are extremely hallucinogenic.

Off-Campus Housing – Housing from a particular landlord or rental group that is not affiliated with the university. Depending on the college, off-campus housing can range from extremely popular to non-existent. Those students who choose to live off campus are typically given more freedom, but they also have to deal with things such as possible subletting scenarios, furniture, and bills. In addition to these factors, rental prices and distance often affect a student's decision to move off campus.

Office Hours – Time that teachers set aside for students who have questions about the coursework. Office hours are a good place for students to go over any problems and to show interest in the subject material.

Pledging – The time after a student has gone through rush, received a bid, and has chosen a particular fraternity or sorority they would like to join. Pledging usually lasts anywhere from one to two semesters. Once the pledging period is complete and a particular student has done everything that is required to become a member, they are considered a brother or sister. If a fraternity or a sorority would decide to "haze" a group of students, these initiation rituals would take place during the pledging period.

Private Institution – A school that does not use taxpayers dollars to help subsidize education costs. Private schools typically cost more than public schools and are usually smaller.

Prof – Slang for "professor."

Public Institution – A school that uses taxpayers dollars to help subsidize education costs. Public schools are often a good value for in-state residents and tend to be larger than most private colleges.

Quarter System (sometimes referred to as the Trimester System) – A type of academic calendar system. In this setup, students take classes for three academic periods. The first quarter usually starts in late September or early October and concludes right before Christmas. The second quarter usually starts around early to mid–January and finishes up around March or April. The last quarter, or "third quarter," usually starts in late March or early April and finishes up in late May or Mid-June. The fourth quarter is summer. The major difference between the quarter system and semester system is that students take more courses but with less coverage.

RA (Resident Assistant) – A student leader who is assigned to a particular floor in a dormitory in order to help to the other students who live there. A RA's duties include ensuring student safety and providing guidance or assistance wherever possible.

Recitation – An extension of a specific course; a "review" session of sorts. Because some classes are so large, recitations offer a setting with fewer students where students can ask questions and get help from professors or TAs in a more personalized environment. As a result, it is common for most large lecture classes to be supplemented with recitations.

Rolling Admissions – A form of admissions. Most commonly found at public institutions, schools with this type of policy continue to accept students throughout the year until their class sizes are met. For example, some schools begin accepting students as early as December and will continue to do so until April or May.

Room and Board – This is typically the combined cost of a university-owned room and a meal plan.

Room Draw/Housing Lottery – A common way to pick on-campus room assignments for the following year. If a student decides to remain in university-owned housing, they are assigned a unique number that, along with seniority, is used to choose their new rooms for the next year.

Rush – The period in which students can meet the brothers and sisters of a particular chapter and find out if a given fraternity or sorority is right for them. Rushing a fraternity or a sorority is not a requirement at any school. The goal of rush is to give students who are serious about pledging a feel for what to expect.

Semester System – The most common type of academic calendar system at college campuses. This setup typically includes two semesters in a given school year. The "fall" semester starts around the end of August or early September and finishes right before winter vacation. The "spring" semester usually starts in mid-January and ends around late April or May.

Student Center/Rec Center/Student Union – A common area on campus that often contains study areas, recreation facilities, and eateries. This building is often a good place to meet up with fellow students and is most commonly used as a hangout. Depending on the school, the student center can have a huge role or a non-existent role in campus life.

Student ID – A university-issued photo ID that serves as a student's key to many different functions within an institution. Some schools require students to show these cards in order to get into dorms, libraries, cafeterias, and other facilities. In addition to storing meal plan information, in some cases, a student ID can actually work as a debit card and allow students to purchase things from bookstores or local shops.

Suite – A type of dorm room. Unlike other places that have communal bathrooms that are shared by the entire floor, a suite has a private bathroom. Suite-style dorm rooms can house anywhere from two to ten students.

TA (Teacher's Assistant) – An undergraduate or grad student who helps in some manner with a specific course. In some cases, a TA will teach a class, assist a professor, grade assignments, or conduct office hours.

Undergraduate – A student who is in the process of studying for their Bachelor (college) degree.

ABOUT THE AUTHOR:

I hope this book provided you with an insider's glance into the world of LMU and Los Angeles. I am now a a sophomore at Loyola Marymount, pursing an English degree with a specialization in Screenwriting, and with hard work, I expect to graduate soon. Eventually, I would like to blaze new trails as one of the few women writing edgy thrillers for the big screen. Although non-fiction is a new world for me, this book allowed me to experiment and expand my writing into a new area. More importantly, the book offered me the chance to explore LMU's past and present and reaffirm why I am here.

This book was my first foray into the publishing world, and I could not have done it without the help of so many wonderful people. First, thanks to the students, staff, and faculty of LMU who filled out surveys, answered questions, and dug up the necessary information to make this project as complete and accurate as possible. Your help was priceless. Thanks to the staff at College Prowler for providing the support and answers to string these words together. Many thanks go out to the staff of Communications and Public Affairs, especially Melissa Abraham. And, of course, much thanks and love to my mom, Ron, and Ronnie for the love and laughs. Last, but certainly not least, my dad, who has always been my biggest fan and is mentally cheering me on through everything. Thanks, Dad.

Kristin Cole

Email the Author at kristencole@collegeprowler.com

Notes

....

....

....

....

....

....

....

....

....

....

....

....

....

Notes

....

....

....

....

....

....

....

....

....

....

....

....

....

....

Notes

....

....

....

....

....

....

....

....

....

....

....

....

....

Need More Help?

Do you have more questions about this school? Can't find a certain statistic? College Prowler is here to help. We are the best source of college information on the planet. We have a network of thousands of students who can get the latest information on any school to you ASAP. E-mail us at *info@collegeprowler.com* with your college-related questions. It's like having an older sibling show you the ropes!

Email Us Your College-Related Questions!

Check out **www.collegeprowler.com** for more details.
1.800.290.2682

Notes

....

....

....

....

....

....

....

....

....

....

....

....

....

Tell Us What Life Is Really Like At Your School!

Have you ever wanted to let people know what your school is really like? Now's your chance to help millions of high school students choose the right school.

Let your voice be heard and win cash and prizes!

Check out **www.collegeprowler.com** for more info!

Notes

....

....

....

....

....

....

....

....

....

....

....

....

....

Do You Have What It Takes To Get Admitted?

The College Prowler Road to College Counseling Program is here. An admissions officer will review your candidacy at the school of your choice and create a 12+ page personal admission plan. We rate your credentials with the same criteria used by school admissions committees. We assess your strengths and weaknesses and create a plan of action that makes a difference.

Check out **www.collegeprowler.com** or call 1.800.290.2682 for complete details.

Notes

....

....

....

....

....

....

....

....

....

....

....

....

....

Pros and Cons

Still can't figure out if this is the right school for you?
You've already read through this in-depth guide; why not
list the pros and cons? It will really help with narrowing down
your decision and determining whether or not
this school is right for you.

Pros	Cons

Notes

....

....

....

....

....

....

....

....

....

....

....

....

....

Need Help Paying For School?

Apply for our Scholarship!

College Prowler awards thousands of dollars a year to students who compose the best essays. E-mail *scholarship@collegeprowler.com* for more information, or call 1.800.290.2682.

Apply now at **www.collegeprowler.com**

Notes

....

....

....

....

....

....

....

....

....

....

....

....

....

Notes

....
....
....
....
....
....
....
....
....
....
....
....
....
....

Notes

....

....

....

....

....

....

....

....

....

....

....

....

....

Notes

....

....

....

....

....

....

....

....

....

....

....

....

....

Write For Us!
Get Published! Voice Your Opinion.

Writing a College Prowler guidebook is both fun and rewarding; our open-ended format allows your own creativity free reign. Our writers have been featured in national newspapers and have seen their names in bookstores across the country. Now is your chance to break into the publishing industry with one of the country's fastest-growing publishers!

Apply now at **www.collegeprowler.com**

Contact *editor@collegeprowler.com* or call 1.800.290.2682 for more details.

Notes

....

....

....

....

....

....

....

....

....

....

....

....

....